THE POLITICAL RACKET

Deceit, Self-Interest and Corruption in American Politics

Also by Martin L. Gross:

The Brain Watchers
The Doctors
The Psychological Society
The Government Racket: Washington Waste from A to Z
A Call for Revolution: How Washington Is Strangling America—and How to Stop It
The Great Whitewater Fiasco: An American Tale of Money, Power, and Politics
The Tax Racket: Government Extortion from A to Z

THE POLITICAL RACKET

Deceit, Self-Interest and Corruption in American Politics

Martin L. Gross

Ballantine Books • New York

 Published in the United States by Ballantine Books, a division of Random House, Inc., New York, and simultaneously in Canada by Random House of Canada Limited, Toronto.

http://www. randomhouse.com

Library of Congress Catalog Card Number: 96-96185

ISBN: 0-345-38777-5

Cover illustration by Sandy Huffaker
Cover design by Michèle Brinson

Manufactured in the United States of America

First Edition: May 1996

10 9 8 7 6 5 4 3 2 1

To my wife, Anita

• • •

"I am a firm believer in the people. If given the truth, they can be depended upon to meet any national crisis. The great point is to bring them the real facts."

—Abraham Lincoln

CONTENTS

1

OUR PROFESSIONAL POLITICIANS

A Citizen Indictment

Never before have Americans been as frustrated about their nation and its political system as they are today.

The people are stricken with doubt—bewildered by what is best called THE MESS: high taxes, stagnant incomes, government waste in multibillions, a weakened middle class, loss of our manufacturing base, poor education, trade deficits, corrupt politics, campaign financing hijinks, failed welfare programs and corporate downsizing.

Even at the depths of the Great Depression, most were sure that America—with its extraordinary past and its youthful optimism—would find its way out of the morass.

But not today. Though economic conditions are much

better than in the 1930s, pessimism is becoming ingrained in the American psyche, and with good cause.

Who's to blame?

Traditionally, Americans look to the source. If a house is poorly constructed, we blame the builder. When a simple medical operation fails, we look to the surgeon. When a car is recalled, we look to the manufacturer.

But when our society and economy become dangerously weakened, as they have today, we place the blame everywhere except where it belongs—on those who govern our overly complex system: the army of 500,000 elected officials, the great majority of whom are PROFESSIONAL POLITICIANS, from mayor to the president of the United States, the shepherds of our 85,000 different governments.

First Do No Harm

Citizens have become unwilling victims of that profession, which, over the past thirty years, has made extravagant promises. Not only have politicians failed to fulfill them, but they have violated the most important rule of any profession: PRIMUM NON NOCERE—First Do No Harm.

There is little doubt that their efforts since the 1960s have damaged the basic structure of political and social life. Politicians work obsessively at serving themselves by raising vast war chests, becoming expert in fanciful rhetoric, then conquering the ballot box.

But they fail miserably in serving the great army of the working middle class who pay the bills, including their often-inflated salaries. Too many politicians march to an internal drummer, one that is seriously out of step with the public's own beat.

One thing is sure: Americans are not sanguine about their government or the two political parties which control it. Three-fourths of voters do not trust Washington to do the right thing on any given occasion. Sixty-four percent do not think America is on the right track. Sixty-two percent would like to see a third party—just to keep the two parties philosophically honest.

More citizens are now registered as independents or "unaffiliated" than as Democrats or Republicans, and the movement away from the major parties is growing. Why? One reason is that the parties are not producing the leaders the nation wants and needs, which explains the enthusiastic reception given to nonpolitician Gen. Colin Powell in 1995.

Why the disillusionment? Because we are beginning to recognize that the people who make the rules are members of a failed profession, and that the structure they have erected is not sound.

The American economy has been stagnating year by year. Our politicians not only refuse to recognize it, but make foolish pronouncements about its strength. In his 1996 State of the Union address, President Clinton used ridiculous hyperbole, proclaiming that the economy was "the healthiest it's been in three decades." His predecessor, George Bush, wore the same economic blinders, apparently a vocational disability of modern Presidents. In the midst of the recession of 1991, he was proclaiming its potency.

Except for the favored, the economic weakness is deep and unyielding.

American workers now net almost 20 percent less in real wages than they did in 1973; we are the only Western nation to have so retrogressed. After taxes, two paychecks in a family barely equal the purchasing power one had twenty-five years ago. The average household income is only $33,000 and going nowhere, bringing America down to eighth place in the world in per capita income.

The gulf between corporate wealth and middle-class penury is spreading, creating a great divide, one which we've never experienced before. During 1995, as Wall Street rose some 35 percent, one of the largest gains in history, the average American *lost* 2 percent in real income.

Crushing the Middle Class

Taxes at all levels, which took 17 percent of the GDP (gross domestic product) under "big spender" FDR, now take 40 percent, crushing the savings and investment possibilities of the middle class. Taxes now eat up more cash in the typical family budget than housing, food and medical care combined. The contrast with the past is shocking. In 1950, the average American family of four paid only $66 in federal income taxes, a mere 2 percent of their earnings.

And today? The social, economic and political climate created by our politicians is eroding the fabric of everyday life.

Manufacturing jobs have been decimated by the national trade policy, which has created enormous trade imbalances with the Asian continent. We have lost 4 million manufacturing slots to overseas in the last decade, with no tourniquet in place to control the bleeding, and apparently little or no interest in the dilemma by either political party.

Meanwhile, the ranks of politicians' first cousin, the government bureaucrat, continue to expand despite the talk of downsizing. There are now 19.5 million Americans working for governments, a million more than in manufacturing. While manufacturing jobs have been static since 1975, government jobs have increased by 5 million.

Politicians talk glibly about cutting taxes. But if the entire Republican wish list—the more generous of the two plans—were to be fully enacted, taxes would still be *higher* in the magical year of 2002 than they are today. Just the automatic yearly FICA tax rise is larger than the miniscule cuts likely to go into effect. Meanwhile, local property and school taxes increase twice as fast as inflation.

(Has anyone quantified the stress and unhappiness in America created by high taxes?)

Employing their quiver of lies, politicians in both parties are now pretending to create a so-called balanced budget by 2002. But even if they "succeed," as we shall see, the budget will be at least $112 billion in the red, counting only the money borrowed (read "stolen") from Social Security.

Most problems in bad government stem from one source: the failings of the contemporary political animal—

circa post-1970. Six of these failings (a full indictment follows later) are:

1. Politicians are less honest and more apt to lie than the typical American.
2. They put too much emphasis on ideology and not enough on pragmatism.
3. Money dominates and distorts the whole political system.
4. In a nation whose Constitution was written to ensure a small federal operation, most politicians seem to have a quasi-religious belief in big government.
5. Self-interest and corruption are too common among politicians.
6. Politicians are dangerously ignorant of the true facts and cost of government.

Champions of the left and right are valuable for crystallizing the arguments, but we've seen how their clashes can destroy civil discourse. Congressman Charles Rangel of New York, a liberal Democrat, recently compared Republican social policies to that of Hitler's treatment of the Jews. Conversely, a Republican "Wanted Poster" of liberals singled out mainly Afro-Americans and women as the main offenders.

Unlike Europe, America has seldom been plagued by extreme ideology—witness the middle-class orientation of Democrat Harry Truman and Republican Dwight Eisenhower. But when the Democratic Party moved left beginning in 1972 with George McGovern, then in 1976 with Jimmy Carter, and again in 1992 with Bill Clinton, the Republican Party reacted by bringing up its own ideological guns and moving strongly to the right.

The result is a growing and crippling class warfare, one which is typically non-American. In some strange way, we are imitating the class conflict of the old British social war—the tussle between the Labour and Conservative Parties, a vise they're desperately trying to break. The difference, of course, is that despite their claims, the Democratic Party is no longer the workingman's party. And the Republican Party, while addressing the problem of monster government and high taxes, avoids other economic problems of the squeezed middle class.

Hole in the Center

The present American political system leaves a giant hole in the center, one which has not been filled by anyone, let alone by our intellectually challenged politicians. This missing center is less about ideology than about pragmatism, once America's trump card. The result is that both political parties, infatuated with their own rhetoric, fail to address the crying needs of most Americans.

In the general indictment, are we talking about *all* politicians? Or *most* politicians? Or only *some* politicians?

The question is not a relevant one. Each profession, movement or class has a *thrust* that illustrates how it operates and marks its influence on society. In the case of the Political Class, that mark—at its worst—is campaign finance corruption, lobbyist pressure, egomania, cronyism, lying, indifference to voter needs, waste and ignorance.

Some politicians courageously escape those sins, but the mark of failure is stamped on the entire profession. In varying degrees, it taints all those involved, with only rare exceptions.

Are politicians different from the people they serve? Are they a special personality type, one which thrives in the modern circus of democracy?

As a group, politicians are not evil, but neither are they a true sample of the population.

F. Scott Fitzgerald assured us that the rich are truly different. Politicians seem to be the same—people somehow removed from the temper and concerns of ordinary citizens. Intellectually, they appear to be no different from the average college-educated American. But emotionally, they tend to seek the limelight, and are willing to suffer the slings of criticism to achieve the equivalent of modern stardom. Are they, we might ask, a brand of entertainer, yet a group with considerably more power than the stellar lights of Hollywood?

That is one purpose of this book: to peer behind the scrim and show the Political Class as it truly is.

The personality of politicians often leaves much to be desired. Some come to believe that they are *übermenschen*, chosen by divine intervention rather than by the simple vote of their fellow citizens. The Greeks call that trait "hubris," and it seems to affect (or infect) too many in the Political Class.

Exaggerated Personae

Over a hundred years ago, poet Walt Whitman spoke of "the never-ending audacity of elected officials." With their constant appearances on television today, the problem of celebrityhood has become even more serious. Some politicians feed off publicity to create an exaggerated personae, one which isolates them from the voters and limits their ability to understand the public's needs and moods.

For many, the special treatment they receive (like a personal parking spot at National Airport for congressmen) convinces them of their importance. The celebrity and perks are taken as proper rewards of their superior station. Even those who come to Washington quite innocent, perhaps naive, often become prisoners of the exaggerated Washington culture.

Hasn't it always been this way?

Never to this extent.

Let's compare today's crowd with politicians of an earlier period, say 1944. Harry Truman was Vice President. He lived in a two-bedroom apartment on upper Connecticut Avenue, for which he paid $140 a month out of his $12,000 yearly salary. His office was a hole-in-the-wall space off the Senate lobby, where he had a total staff of four.

And today? Whether Republican Dan Quayle or Democrat Al Gore, the vice presidency has assumed the aura of royalty.

They have a staff of sixty-five people. *Marilyn* Quayle had a government staff larger than Harry Truman's. (Mrs. Gore's office won't talk.) They live in a mansion on the grounds of the Naval Observatory, which we're renovating for $3.5 million, including $278,000 for the "veranda," apparently southern for "porch."

Their taxpayer largesse includes a $50,000-a-year housekeeper, a Navy crew to take care of the house and grounds, a fleet of cars, three drivers, a Boeing 707 jet and a $90,000 annual entertainment allowance. Al Gore, breaking all records, has five—count them: five—offices, including one in his home state of Tennessee, a perk never even contemplated by other VPs, or anyone else.

Little wonder that Harry Truman (like Gore, a Democrat), who left office with little in the bank and no federal pension, is now a folk hero.

Those Happy Junkets

One politician excess is free vacationing on the taxpayer's nickel, or, more likely, hundreds of thousands of dollars. These federal "junkets," as the freebies are called, are an increasingly popular form of extravagance. The rationale, which is generally as false as a $3 bill, is that they're going on "fact-finding" missions to Hong Kong or Paris. Surprisingly, they need their spouses along, probably to take notes.

During the 1995 Christmas season, when much of the government was closed for lack of funds, twenty-five members of Congress sought to use government planes to go on junkets around the world. (We run a giant boondoggle for this, the 89th Military Airlift, the "Airline of the VIPs," out of Andrews Air Force Base, eleven miles from Washington.)

One three-continent junketeer, Republican Senator Arlen Specter of Pennsylvania, even had the State Department wire ahead to set up squash partners for him on air-conditioned courts!

But haven't politicians always been mocked and held in some disrepute?

True. Will Rogers called members of Congress "America's only native criminal class." Back in 1835, Alexis de Tocqueville, on his historic six-month tour of America, wrote of the relative inferiority of most members of the House.

But whether their inferiority is exaggerated or not, their power was much less important then than it is now. Government was small and early Americans paid almost no taxes. Most of the money to run Washington came from tariffs paid by foreign businessmen. Nor did the government usually engage in projects beyond the ability of its pocketbook or the intelligence of its politicians, as we routinely do today. Government now virtually controls our lives, and those who control the government, at all levels, are obviously not equal to the task.

The result—bad, expensive government—surrounds us, from poor education tolerated by governors and school boards to continual crisis—financial, logical and moral—in Washington.

Witness the failed economic growth rate of the nation. A generation ago in the 1960s, it averaged 4.4 percent, but in the 1990s, it has been stalled at an anemic 1.8 percent level, a formula for stagnation and worse. Within fifteen years, the Social Security System (whose annual $70 billion surplus is taken and spent in the general fund) will need massive infusions of cash from new FICA taxes or increased government borrowing if the baby boomers are not to end up as the prime suckers of the twenty-first century.

The Potent Politician

Meanwhile, the Political Class has never been stronger.

They raise their salaries faster than those of voters. They defy the wishes of the people by defeating "term limits" in Congress. (Yes, it's in the "Contract.") In twenty-three states, they have sued and overturned voter Initiatives for term limits for members of Congress. They refuse to grant the Initiative and Referendum to citizens in most states. They insist on a multitude of perks and privileges. They resist true reform at almost every level.

But they take very good care of themselves. Pensions of politicians, which can reach into the millions, continue to outpace those of the populace. Defeated former speaker Tom Foley is retired to Washington State on $123,800 a year plus a taxpayer-paid suite and a staff of three, all courtesy of the superfluous Office of Former Speakers. We see that same excess among government bureaucrats. In New York, a Port Authority executive recently retired with a pension of $117,000 a year, an insult to Big Apple taxpayers.

MONEY is corrupting American politics at every level. Political campaign chests continue to fill to the brim. In 1996, politicians of all stripes will raise and spend an extravagant (even obscene) $1.5 billion for their elections. In the presidential race, taxpayers alone will cough up $40 million for the primaries, then $60 million for each of the major party candidates, much of it for television advertising that distorts their opponent's records. We even pay $12 million to each party to hold their circuslike conventions, confetti and all.

In the 1996 Republican Presidential primaries, by

March 1, $138 million had been spent by the candidates as opposed to just $23 million in the 1992 primaries.

The cost of congressional campaigns continues to escalate. It has reached to heights of over $5 million for House seats, and $28 million for a Senate seat. Even some state legislature races have passed the $1 million barrier. In many cases, the money raised is just thinly disguised "legal bribery," gifts from special interests in return for favors already given, or those promised.

(What some politicians blithely consider "campaign contributions" may actually be criminal bribes or "illegal gratuities," as a few prosecutors are successfully claiming [see Chapter 3].)

Sometimes the smallest cash grease can help accomplish wonders for creative lobbyists in pursuit of favorable legislation. In New York, the beverage industry hosted a $1,397 dinner for Republican state leaders at the five-star Lutèce restaurant. Minding their bipartisanship, the industry regaled Democratic leaders at the Four Seasons at a $2,354 meal. Without making a direct connection, a *New York Times* editorial pointed out that the industry had received a $42 million tax cut.

Buying Allegiance

Only very rich politicians who finance their own campaigns escape the chasing of tainted, sometimes illegal, funds. But these wealthy candidates distort democracy by trying to buy our allegiance, using their private bankrolls to gain advantage over those who must beg for their political porridge.

Witness the 1994 senatorial campaign of Michael

Huffington in California, which ate up $28 million of his own cash, and the 1996 presidential campaign of Republican Steve Forbes. Despite being almost unknown to the public, the wealthy publisher initially moved smartly ahead in the primaries by spending $25 million in the first month, mainly on thirty-second television ads.

When personal wealth is not available, friendly banks can fill in. Witness the $3.5 million loan in 1992 to Democrat Bill Clinton from the Worthen Bank in Little Rock, money that was poured into an avalanche of television ads for the Super Tuesday primaries that put him over.

MONEY is a major root of American political failure. Wherever there's too much of it, whether in the Mafia, Hollywood or Washington, excess and corruption inevitably follow. The 4,016 PACs with enormous war chests from special interests can dispense up to $10,000 each to any politician who sides with them, or who they believe can be wooed.

No country has as convoluted a system of political corruption as does America. But only a few Washingtonians plead guilty to political whoring to get the money needed to mount their campaigns. Others cry out in response: "It's true, but we're getting religion. We're reforming."

Nonsense. Lobbyists are the source of a substantial piece of the money, but the lobbying reform bill recently passed by Congress, for instance, is nearly worthless. It merely requires that the army of paid persuaders must register and disclose how much money they've targeted for what cause. Meanwhile, their ranks multiply mightily, not only in Washington but in state capitals as well (see Chapter 7).

Present reform ideas, whether on lobbying, ethics, elections or campaign finance, are far behind the curve, and are mainly designed to divert the public from true change. As we shall see, they are mainly wish-fulfillments that do not come to grips with either the need to clean house or to shore up the weak structure of American politics. Numerous "reform" bills are wending their way through Congress, but true reform is not on the congressional or presidential horizon, though we shall give it a shot in this volume.

Ear of the President

No reform now contemplated will stop the most sophisticated of the influence-peddlers—the lawyer/lobbyists—from getting the ear of the powerful, including the president of the United States, regardless of party.

That influence was once in the hands of veteran lawyer/lobbyist Clark Clifford, who was the confidant of Presidents Truman, Kennedy, Johnson and Carter. Unfortunately, he yielded to the Washington siren song and ended his career in disgrace in connection with the BCCI scandal.

Another phenomenon that increasingly shapes the jaded Beltway culture is the highly paid political consultant, the hired gun of modern mythmakers, from mayors to the president of the United States (see Chapter 7). Supposed experts on everything from polling to direct-mail fund-raising, to television commercials, to advice to politicians, their ranks include such stars as Republican Ed

Rollins (noted for hoof-in-mouthery) and the latest rage, Dick Morris.

Morris has worked for both parties and is the éminence grise in the White House who smoothly orchestrated President Clinton's reshaping of himself as a dedicated centrist for the November 1996 election.

Politics in America is dissected every Sunday morning on television, but *politicians* have miraculously escaped the journalistic microscope. While a handful may be called to task, politicians in general have escaped examination and indictment.

Their errant behavior is treated only anecdotally, as if each deceitful, inept or corrupt politician is a single case history that bears no relation to their colleagues. In reality, they are closely related in attitude and performance, and mostly products of the statehouse and Washington (Beltway) cultures.

Without that examination, the failings of their trade will not only continue but accelerate.

What is that indictment? What do they do that erodes the structural strength of the country?

The indictment is long and deep, as we shall see. But the overall charge is that American politicians are guilty of wholesale mismanagement of the nation, its economy, its goals, its resources, its talents and its basic stability.

Americans may not know the details, but they intuitively sense that *something* has gone wrong. Among twenty-five professions, for instance, members of Congress rank twenty-fourth in a poll (pharmacists are first) in reputation for honesty.

Perfect Prevaricators

Little wonder that lies from the Political Class are not only commonplace but expected. In fact, politics is the only profession where prevarication is routine.

Former president George Bush asked us to "read his lips" only to sign into law one of the largest tax raises in history. While campaigning, President Clinton assured us of a middle-class tax cut, only to raise gas taxes for all, increase Social Security taxes for millions and impose a giant tax raise on the large upper middle class who are falsely called "rich" but who play a vital role in maintaining a healthy economy with their consumption and investment.

Politicians of both parties, working semi-secretly in the House Ways and Means Committee, have for the past thirty years regularly lowered deductions—from personal exemptions to interest on loans to sales taxes—on our Form 1040s, creating enormous unseen tax hikes.

Rhetoric has replaced reality in politics. Politicians, including the President, have recently been talking about "the end of big government" with its waste and inefficiency. The reality is quite the opposite. From 1992, when the debate truly began (the year of the Perot movement and the publication of my book *The Government Racket: Washington Waste from A to Z*), the size of the federal government has grown almost 5 percent per year, twice as rapidly as inflation. Many local and state governments have increased even more swiftly.

Even if the so-called tough Republican balanced budget plan had been adopted, which it hasn't, Washington budgets would still grow 3.5 percent per year, less than the Democratic plan but more than inflation. By both parties figures, the national debt will grow to $6 trillion by the year 2002.

The reality? Big government—at the federal, state and local levels—is thoroughly entrenched and getting larger all the time despite the political rhetoric on either side of the aisle.

Epidemic Corruption

Another political sin, criminal corruption, sometimes seems epidemic. Large numbers of politicians, from mayors to congressmen, are convicted each year for bribery and campaign finance violations. Corruption ranges from as lofty a height as the vice president's office down to the mayors of small towns.

VP Spiro Agnew, whose statue was recently unveiled in a Senate corridor, pleaded nolo contendere and resigned in 1973 after he was indicted for receiving envelopes stuffed with cash from builders in his home state of Maryland. In little Naugatuck, Connecticut, Mayor William C. Rado was convicted for taking bribes from a construction company and served two months in jail.

(Maybe Americans are too forgiving. In 1995, the townspeople not only forgave Rado but elected him mayor again as an Independent. We shouldn't forget that Mayor James Curley, a Boston legend, ran the city from his jail cell.)

Some politicians escape legal punishment while distorting the law. Republican Utah Congresswoman Enid Waldholtz, who broke a multitude of campaign finance rules, to the tune of over $1 million, wailed for four hours that "her husband did it."

Ethics committees in Congress, as well as state legislatures, fail to properly oversee the morality of their members. Gary Ruskin of the Congressional Accountability Project calls them "Member Protection Committees." We're learning that campaign contributions can buy more than a "thank you," and that cronyism can conquer civic responsibility.

Democratic minority leader Tom Daschle of South Dakota was recently exonerated by the Senate Ethics Committee of charges that he intervened in the regulation of the airworthiness of a charter airline owned by a friend. One of its planes crashed soon after, killing its passengers and crew. It was excused away as "constituent service," the same claim made by a Democratic senator involved in the Keating Five S & L scandal who was subsequently chastised by his legislative body.

In New York State, Republican Governor George Pataki was ostensibly dismayed to learn that one of his chief fund-raisers was also involved in handing out state contracts, a perfect setup for filling party coffers. In Travelgate, when a big Clinton contributor, Harry Thomason, sought to get the White House travel account, seven innocent public servants were discharged.

Favors from the Senate

Hidden corruption among prominent politicians surfaces in the most unexpected ways. Former Republican Senator Bob Packwood was considered a fiscally honorable if a kissing-fool politician. But his eight-hundred-page private diary (shades of the self-incriminating Nixon tapes) revealed that he not only was involved in a secret $100,000 campaign contribution, an action he thought could be considered a "felony," but was also a willing patsy for friendly lobbyists who came calling with checks.

One of the cleverest explanations of how the system of lobbyist cash works came in a comment by former congressman Peter Kostmayer of Pennsylvania: "I remember when I got on the Energy and Commerce, everybody jumped for the Telecommunications Subcommittee first. . . . There was a member sitting next to me, and every time another member bid for that subcommittee, he went 'Ding'—as if the cash register was going off."

In the Executive Branch, Clinton cabinet members in Agriculture, Energy, Transportation and Commerce have been investigated for their alleged errant behavior. (Was that because "they looked like America"?)

Hazel O'Leary of Energy was implicated in taking atrociously expensive overseas trips with her staff. After a Special Counsel investigation, Secretary Mike Espy of Agriculture resigned for accepting "gifts" and had to return $7,600 in expenses.

Insensitive politicians find ingenious ways to cash in. Republican Senator Alfonse D'Amato managed to make $37,000 in one day by buying and selling an initial public offering (IPO) of stock reserved for better customers and the well placed. Likewise, former Democratic Speaker of the House Tom Foley was a master of friendly IPOs provided for him by a Boston brokerage house. His take of $100,000 was even larger, perhaps a matter of seniority.

No More, Please

Some politicians are beginning to react to the failure of their profession. In 1996, thirteen senators and twenty-seven House members declared that they were not running for reelection, the greatest mass defection since 1896.

Why? The wearying nature of fund-raising, the ideological battle, the excessive complexity of government, the lack of civil discourse and the growing disrespect of the public have taken the thrill out of politics for many.

Plato has told us that people tend to do that which the community honors. Since too many politicians consider Washington their community, they are behaving as poorly as many of their colleagues. If the broader community, the public, is to be wooed back into respecting their public servants, there must be soul-searching among politicians, and a change of system that goes far beyond the current, often childish, "reforms."

Another failing of self-serving American politicians—compulsive about raising money and running for office—is that they are often quite ignorant of the true facts and costs of government.

Congressmen commonly speak about the cost of "welfare," for instance, as anywhere from $20 to $60 billion. The reality is explained in a Congressional Research Service catalogue of welfare called "Cash and Non-Benefits for People of Limited Income."

The true figure is $400 billion a year—three-fourths of it federal money—for eighty programs to feed, house, clothe, heal and educate the poor, a larger expenditure than even defense. Perhaps we should spend that much, but congressmen pass welfare legislation for six cabinet agencies with no knowledge of its true cost. (Neither does it appear in the federal budget document, cost $45.)

At least twice, I brought up this information while testifying before Congress, only to receive blank stares from members.

Nor does it help when the government issues false statistical reports. They may assuage our fears but they give out distorted information to our politicians, who usually find it hard to keep up anyway.

Jiggered Figures

A case in point is the unemployment rate. The Bureau of Labor Statistics (BLS) regularly reports a 5.4 to 5.7 percent figure, which is considered almost full employment. Of course, the number is a blatant lie.

It counts only those who are actively looking for a job that month, a ridiculous and fake method of scoring those out-of-work.

How many people are actually unemployed who are not included in the government's fictitious statistics? There are 5.8 million people who want a job but are not working for any number of reasons—yet are magically not unemployed as far as the BLS is concerned. Among them are 1.7 million people who are considered "Marginally Attached"—a cruel euphemism for those without a paycheck and whose unemployment insurance has run out. They are not working but they are *not counted as unemployed* because they didn't look for work that month!

There are also 409,000 "Discouraged Workers" who want a job badly, and who did look for work within twelve months. But they didn't look for work that month because they didn't think they could find it. These unfortunate people, who are among the most desperate of the unemployed, are not counted as unemployed because the government knows that their despair would further spoil the government's falsely rosy numbers.

Few of the 5 million family heads on welfare are working, but welfare recipients are not counted as unemployed.

We're now up to much higher numbers of unemployed than the fictional 5.5 percent. *BUT wait*, there's a lot more chicanery in the federal deception. There are 4.1 million part-time workers who want, but can't find, a full-time job. They are counted as if they were fully employed. Then there are 2.1 million temps working that month who are counted as fully employed. Then there are the millions laid off and "downsized" who might be living on their severance pay or savings, or eeking out a pittance as so-called self-employed. They're not counted as unemployed either.

Does the government have a semi-secret number they hide that's a little closer to the truth?

Yes. They combine the 5.5 percent from their doctored survey, then add those who work part-time because they can't get a regular job, plus the "Marginally Attached" super-unemployed, all of which gives us a closer-to-the-truth unemployment figure.

What is it?

According to the BLS it was 10.8 percent in January 1996. BUT the BLS, who work for the politicians in the White House (of whatever administration), make sure that that disheartening figure is not included in the written part of their press release. It is buried in copious tables, which easily fools the media.

What, then, is the real, real number of the unemployed in America?

Well, if you just take the 10.8 percent, and add the "Discouraged" and the remaining 3.7 million out-of-work not counted, you come closer to 15 percent, which is nearer to the true figure. That doesn't include people on welfare, which would add another 3 percent or so.

It's probable that America now has the highest unemployment in the Western industrial world. Lester Thurow, the renowned MIT economist comes up with the same 15 percent on his own, confirmation of the mathematically obvious.

In February 1996, there was a quick flurry of optimism when the BLS reported over 700,000 new jobs, only to be followed with the deflating news that most were part-time, temp and near–minimum wage positions—the new trend in American "employment."

The politicians expect us to trust their word, but most know less about unemployment than the man-in-the-street, whose instincts tell him the government figures were fake to begin with.

Little wonder the rhetoric of government and politicians rings hollow to citizens who sense the truth.

Is the politician or the system at fault?

Actually, it's both. It's like nature and nuture combining to create a mix that's either beneficial or harmful. The political system was set up for another era, when it worked well. But its structure is now broken. The expansion of population, television, big money, the army of lobbyists, the crazy quilt primary system, consultants and other pressing factors have made our political system an anachronism—technological yet unwieldy, modern and archaic, all at the same time.

The result?

An increasingly distorted political methodology which often encourages the wrong type of politician, with the wrong attitude toward his fellow citizens, promoted and elected in the wrong way.

The current system cannot *work in the modern world. It brings out the worst in our politicians and is incapable of implementing the needs of the public.*

How to Win by Losing

Because of the outmoded Electoral College system and the surprising absence of a runoff system, for instance, we are the only country in the world where presidents can be inaugurated after losing the election. President Clinton, who garnered only 43 percent of the vote, won 68 percent of the Electoral College and was elected. That same system has similarly failed us ten other times in our history.

Why? Because the system doesn't require a majority for election. It also penalizes independents and third parties. Candidates who might get 49 percent of the vote in a state receive *no* electoral votes in the mostly "winner take all" states. Naturally they're seen as "spoilers." Their votes are wasted, and might even throw the election to someone they don't want. The solution is simple, as we shall see (in my draft twenty-eighth amendment to the Constitution) and requires *immediate* implementation.

Our presidential primary system is a madhouse of fifty different laws, with each state childishly vying to be first and most potent in chosing the nominee. Few states have the same rule, and comparing the results of primaries is like counting chickens and canaries.

In Virginia, as in many states, anyone can vote in the Republican primary. In New Hampshire, both Republicans and Independents can vote in the Republican primary. In Connecticut, only Republicans can vote in the Republican primary. In the Iowa caucuses, not only do you have to show up and stay for a few hours in order to vote, but you can become a Republican that very night, whether or not you were a Democrat or an Independent yesterday! And you can revert to your former registration the next morning.

In New York State, home of the old Tammany Hall, laws virtually require that Republican candidates for president kiss the boss's ring. As failed candidate Pat Buchanan commented in 1996, it's easier to enroll for office in Moscow than in New York State, where Republican Party officials backed Bob Dole. Only the intervention of the courts placed opposing candidates on the primary ballot.

The two parties, which had once served us so well, are failing us. Now mainly trade unions for politicians, they're much to blame for the system's poor performance.

Private Parties

Set up as private organizations in the District of Columbia, these parties have established restrictive rules for primaries and elections, and use the state legislators as their lackeys to keep most citizens out of government.

To participate in politics, people have to join one of the two "clubs" and perform according to their arcane rules and rituals. Increasingly, it seems as if the parties "are" the government, taking over rights and privileges that should belong to the people.

(In Congress, over three hundred party workers in such groups as the Democratic Caucus and the Republican Conference are actually on the federal payroll!)

Rather than rise in life and then decide to serve the nation, politicians must instead rise in these provincial groups by kowtowing to the leaders. If not, there's little chance of their running for major public office—unless they can provide their own large war chest. It's little wonder that candidates offered up by the parties in recent years, especially for the presidency, are often lacking in quality.

To suit themselves, the parties have set rules that are antique, restrictive, eccentric and usually antidemocratic. They are designed to maintain the exclusive nature of the two parties and to keep out interlopers.

Why does it take almost a million signatures for an independent candidate for president to get on the ballot in fifty states today when it took only 40,000 for Bob La Follette to run as an independent in 1924? In Florida, not only does it require 200,000 signatures to get on a statewide ballot, a virtually impossible barrier for an independent, but the candidate has to pay the state ten cents a name.

The answer to this and other gnawing questions is twofold: the Political Class and the Political System. Together, they deliver a double whammy to the nation and democracy. If we are ever to understand, and correct, the failings and follies of our politicians, we need to enumerate them for all to see and study.

Here, then, is a twenty-point Bill of Indictment, a description of the Political Racket that is damaging America.

1. Politicians lie so regularly to achieve their goal of election, or reelection, that the habit often becomes reflexive and pathological.

2. Politicians have become compulsive about raising money for their campaigns. Increasingly, they spend more time and energy on that than in representing the people.

3. Campaign financing, which has reached an obscene level, borders on legal bribery. Money received often represents payments for favors either in the future or for those already done.

4. Paid campaign consultants, who will often work for either side, are the new "hired guns" of politics.

5. The distorted "negative" political advertising on television and radio is a national shame.

6. Too many politicians try to become media "stars," joining in the superficial celebrity culture.

7. There is too much unethical behavior and true corruption in the political system. A disproportionate number of politicians run afoul of the law.

8. Too many politicians "cash in" on their celebrityhood in various, and ingenious, ways.
9. Weak conflict-of-interest laws enable politicians to line their own pockets and get away with it.
10. Excessively high pensions and numerous perks and privileges encourage politicians to become "professionals."
11. Politicians actively resist term limits. Former speaker Tom Foley actually sued the State of Washington for passing such a law.
12. There are too many lawyers in both the Political Class and in the nation's capital. (The D.C. Bar Association had 1,000 members in 1950 and has 65,000 today!)
13. Lobbyists flourish at every level, from the White House to the Town Hall, offering PAC money, even more, in exchange for influence.
14. Politicians regularly cash in as lobbyists, often at double their public salary.
15. Ignorance of the details of legislation is commonplace among members of Congress and state legislatures, who seldom read or understand the bills they pass.
16. The party system dampens individuality and forces politicians to become puppets of their leadership.
17. Political patronage is alive and well in the cities, the statehouses, Congress and the White House.
18. The two parties have treated independents as

second-class citizens, both in exercising the primary vote and in running for office.

19. The laws established by party politicians keep the most talented Americans from running for public office.

20. The Initiative and Referendum, which would transfer some power back to the people, is vigorously opposed by most professional politicians.

Inadequate Professionals

Democracy is the finest gift that organized society can grant to its citizens. To see it perverted by a poor political system that spawns inadequate professionals is an insult to the integrity of our Founding Fathers.

We continually speak of "reform," yet very little changes, and what does usually worsens the situation. There's an old cliché attributed to a nineteenth-century Frenchman, Joseph de Maistre, that "Every nation has the government it deserves."

I hate to believe that's true, for the trusting and hard-working American people deserve better.

The political drama has always been an exaggeration of life in America. The problem is aggravated today by placing our politicians in the hothouse of the Washington environment, where fame, the glare of television and the enormous power granted to the president, the members of Congress, the staff and the hired bureaucrats often creates a distortion of personality, a heightening of vanity, ego and hubris.

The result is a kind of mental instability among

those in the political ranks, a factor that can brutally affect those who breath Washington's air and adopt its peculiar habits. In many cases, the ailment spreads to the statehouses.

Unfortunately, those involved have excessive control over us. They bring their instability directly into our lives, increasing our anxiety about the present and the future.

Begin a Rollback

Our best defense is to set up strict rules of behavior for politicians and rules of engagement with the public lest their control and instability become even more damaging. Since that has already happened to an excessive degree, we must not only rein in the Political Class but roll back their influence as well.

If we are to reinstitute our heritage, there is only one possibility—*radical restructuring of the system.* We need to promote, not dampen, democracy by reducing the power of professional politicians and shut down their opportunity for corruption, legal or otherwise, and their intrusion into our lives, our pocketbooks and our psyches.

These changes, some requiring constitutional amendments which I will outline, will undoubtedly be savagely fought by the Political Class. But they are necessary if we are to ensure the future of the nation.

To that goal, this book is dedicated.

Steady your nerves and read on.

2

THE CAMPAIGN FINANCE RACKET

"Buddy, Can You Spare $100,000?"

In the heat of the summer of 1995, in a desperate search for money to win reelection for President Clinton, the Democratic National Committee came up with what they considered a brilliant scheme. They would sell dinners with President Clinton for $100,000 each, with a few other perks thrown in for dessert.

Don Fowler and Senator Chris Dodd of Connecticut, co-chairmen of the Democratic National Committee, were the midwives at the birth of this extraordinary money-raiser. In capital letters in a solicitation note, potential contributors were told that for a gift of $100,000, they could become a "MANAGING TRUSTEE" of the campaign.

The inducements, outlined in a colorful brochure, were seductive to those drawn to power like a drowning man to a life raft.

- For $100,000, contributors would receive not just one but *two* meals (apparently either breakfast, lunch or dinner) with President Clinton; two more meals with Vice President Gore; a slot on a trade mission to a foreign nation, flown there with Democratic party leaders on the old Air Force One; two "policy retreats" with top administration people; plus perhaps the most enticing perk of all: an assigned Democratic National Committee staffer who would act as gofer to fulfill the fat cat's "personal requests" in Washington.
- For $50,000, contributed or raised, they would receive less, but still get a "reception" with the President; *one* dinner with Al Gore; two high-level briefings on the state of the union; and VIP treatment at the 1996 Democratic convention.
- The poor $10,000 contributor. What could he possibly get? A multiperson reception with the President and "preferred status" at the convention. And, yes, dinner with Al Gore. (Was no one considering Mr. Gore's waistline?)
- You say you have only $1,000 to contribute? If you're a woman, don't worry. The DNC has arranged a booby prize. You will be invited to the distaff side of politics, including a reception with Hillary Rodham Clinton, Tipper Gore and the female appointees of the administration.

Sleaze?

Obviously. But it's especially poignant considering Mr. Clinton's hollow promises to clean up Washington. Said the new chief executive at the end of the "People's Inaugural," which incidentally cost $34 million: "Let us resolve to reform our politics, so that power and privilege no longer shout down the voice of the people. . . . Let's give this capital back to the people to whom it belongs."

During the campaign, he was just as vociferous, promising to "break thc stranglehold of special interests." American politics, he pontificated, "is being held hostage by big money interests . . . and cliques of $100,000 donors buy access to Congress and the White House."

The President did return the capital to the "people," but apparently the people he was speaking of were those "$100,000 donors" who could afford to break croissants with him.

(The scoop, a copy of the "menu" letter that was part of the drive to raise $66 million for the 1996 campaign, was obtained by Lynn Sweet of the Washington bureau of the *Chicago-Sun Times* and followed up by the *Washington Times.* After her exposé, nothing much happened. Then, as others picked it up, the DNC got defensive; then the President nervously ordered a donor perk review. Then, five weeks after Ms. Sweet's exposé, Clinton claimed that the DNC would no longer offer "guaranteed access," although he would still meet with large contributors. Nothing changed except the semantics.)

The Republican National Committee was quick to react to the Democratic money gambit, and immediately criticized them for "selling access" to the White House, which was quite true. So, does the GOP Elephant have more integrity than the Democrat Donkey? Surely the Republican criticism must be accompanied by some hint of higher ethics than their fork-tongued opponents. Right?

Republican Perk Package

Wrong. Back in 1992, the Republicans offered a perk package that was no slouch either. For $92,000 contributed or raised, you got a "photo op" with President Bush, lunch with Dan, breakfast with GOP congressional leaders and a reception with cabinet members. Not bad for less than $100,000.

The 1996 campaign is not far behind in stimulating the flow of cash.

In a near duplicate of the DNC footwork, the RNC reportedly imitated, perhaps even bested, the Clinton fiasco of selling the presidency to the highest bidders. On January 24, 1996, at the redecorated Washington Armory, replete with two giant video screens, they raised an all-time record of $16.3 million in one night. Over 3,000 people attended, paying $1,000 a table for individuals and $1,500 a table for corporate entities.

But the math doesn't add up. All those table purchases barely account for less than $2 million. Where did the *real* money, the rest of the $16 million, come from?

From the same type of people, those who wanted to buy the selling of the president and its chance to rub shoulders, press the flesh, be photographed alongside and pass the salt with the leaders of the free world. According to a story by a Washington reporter for the *New York*

Times, "chief among the inducements was a promise of special access to important House and Senate committee members and private meetings with House Speaker Newt Gingrich and Senate Majority Leader Bob Dole. . . ."

The big prize? For $250,000, says the *Times*, the top contributors were promised a private breakfast with the Republican presidential nominee of 1996!

(The RNC says the reporter misinterpreted the word "private." To them, they claim, it could mean as many as two hundred people.)

Soaring Eagles

The Republicans have no intention of letting a good gimmick lapse. They have formed a plan for continuous injection of cash-for-perks that extends far beyond that glorious January night. It's called the "Eagles Club," and it promises that, like Clinton, they will sell you a piece of the White House *if* the Republicans retake it in 1996. The expectation is that this will raise an additional $14.5 million for the campaign.

Only one thing can be said for the Republicans: Since they were out of office in 1995, they came much cheaper than the Democratic President. Membership in the Eagles costs only $15,000, plus an additional $5,000 for a member's spouse. (With cultural conservatism, the Repubs did not mention "significant others.")

What does that modest sum buy? What access, proximity and perks are they selling?

The items were much like those in the Democratic offer, including special trade mission junkets, a "personal representative" in Washington, meetings with party wheels, special seating at the 1996 convention in San Diego and, *if* their candidate won, VIP treatment at the inauguration and a meeting with the new president and vice president.

The GOP had another inducement the Dems couldn't offer. Rich jocks could participate in President Gerald Ford's tennis and golf tournament in Rancho Mirage, California!

What's it worth? To a political junkie or name dropper, it's a "drop dead" coup. Particularly good for a paltry $20,000, especially when compared to the Dems $100,000 cutoff. But of course the best part, sharing in the victory, was like a crap game, strictly on the *Come*.

But there's one thing missing. In defending his program, RNC chairman Haley Barbour pointed out that they are not selling a dinner with the president. So much for gastronomic politics.

Common Cause, which picketed the Republican fund-raiser, also criticized President Clinton's dinner-for-sale. In a letter to the President, Ann McBride of Common Cause said: "We strongly urge you to end this blatant peddling of access to your Presidency."

Declaration of War

A DNC spokesman spoke of the dispute as if it were a war. "Until the system is changed," said Don Fowler of the DNC, "we will not unilaterally disarm."

Tony Blankley, Newt Gingrich's press secretary, played virginal when he used a more colorful phrase that really described both parties. Speaking of the Dems, he said: "We know what you are. We're just haggling over the price."

Whoredom? The public thinks so, and is aghast that neither party can see themselves as the public does: as influence peddlers who corrupt sacred public offices. A recent poll showed that 83 percent of Americans want the campaign money system changed.

(Would Jefferson and Hamilton be proud of the political parties they have wrought?)

Money has turned American elections into a system of legalized corruption. "Money doesn't talk, it shouts," says political scientist Tom Cronin. Adds Fred Wertheimer, former president of Common Cause: "When you add up all the influence money flowing in Washington in all the various ways, you end up with a corrupting way of life—and citizens know it."

"Every day, millions of dollars are spent in Washington to manipulate public policies to private ends," says Charles Lewis of the Center for Public Integrity. "Money fuels a mercenary culture which is corroding the very foundations of this democracy."

The level of tolerance for campaign corruption is growing. Just a few years ago, less obnoxious money-making schemes sent Washington reeling in indignation. When former treasury secretary Lloyd Bentsen set up a $10,000-a-head breakfast club for lobbyists, he was roundly criticized by everyone, including his own party. "I didn't anticipate the perception," he said, apologizing.

In retrospect, his mistake was selling access to his Senate seat too cheaply. Had he charged $100,000, like the President did, it would have achieved the dignity now associated with big-time immorality.

A New Low

Campaign finance in the United States has reached a new high in low-down finagling. After Watergate, pompous predictions were made about the "reform" that was going to change the system. No more would cash be delivered to politicians, including the President, in envelopes.

Now, twenty years later, what have the reforms achieved?

Nothing. Actually, that would be a favorable judgment. The truth is that the post-Watergate cleansing brought in a kind of moral corruption that has been made quite legal.

The dilemma for politicians was this: How do we set up a reform system with enough built-in loopholes to fool a gullible public? The answer was the most convoluted, piously corrupt system in the history of politics. When viewed in its entirety, it makes one feel nostalgic about the relatively small amounts of cash passed under the table in the regimes of Mayor Curley of Boston and New York's Boss Tweed.

Believe it or not, it goes something like this.

There are two sets of campaign finance laws. One gives the appearance of propriety; the other is an open sesame for corruption, much like the "cooked books" of white-collar criminals.

The first one makes Americans feel virtuous because it places *strict* limits on individual and corporate contributions to candidates. You and I can contribute only

$1,000 in the primary and another $1,000 in the general election to each candidate, for a limit of $25,000 in any election for all candidates.

And corporations? In this supposedly sanctimonious system, contributions from corporations are totally outlawed! Called "hard money," they can't give a single dollar to a candidate lest he look at them kindly.

Sounds good? Surely. But here's the first of several loopholes. The very same corporations can set up Political Action Committees (PACs) to pool money from their employees and managers, then give it, in up to $10,000 hunks, to any candidate. And the watchdog Federal Elections Commission (FEC) keeps an eagle eye out for offenders.

What could be cleaner?

The only problem is that it's a total fraud.

Hard and Soft

In a corrupt legal twist, there's a second set of campaign laws that circumvents the entire "hard money" business. This lets us do whatever we want, and totally within the law. We can be righteous and crooked at the same time, much like the open speakeasies in the era of Prohibition.

Under this peculiar second law, anyone—individuals and corporations alike—can give all they want, with no limits, to any political party!

Called "soft money" (probably because it's got such a nice touch), it totals $200 million a year and should properly be called "sleazy money."

Individuals can give up to $20,000 to the party for its federal account, but they can also give *unlimited* amounts to the nonfederal, or state, accounts of the party. Corporations don't have any limit, and its tissue-soft money goes directly in the nonfederal bank account of the parties.

In this convoluted selling of influence, the only restriction is that the millions in soft money can't be tagged *directly* for a candidate. The $200 million per year is supposed to be used for "getting out the vote" and "party building." These euphemisms mean anything the parties want them to mean, from paying staff salaries, to direct-mail pieces and postage, to high-priced consultants, to television ads asking people to vote "Democratic" or "Republican" rather than for John Doe.

As if voters don't know who's running for president. Who do they think they're kidding?

Expensive Politics

This affront to democracy has become truly big business.

The corporate givers read like a Fortune 500 list—everyone from Bell Atlantic to Philip Morris to AT&T to TCI, the giant cable firm, to Atlantic Richfield and on and on, ad nauseum.

Sony plays both sides of the street, giving $100,000 to the Democrats and $130,000 to the Republicans. (Will Bill Clinton overlook the discrepancy?) Gallo wines has donated over a million dollars to both parties, hedging their bets. It has paid off handsomely. Gallo has received a ridiculous Department of Agriculture subsidy (which I detailed in 1992) of $23.8 million so they can advertise their wines overseas—a 23-to-1 return on their political wager.

Goldman, Sachs and Company, the giant investment

banking firm, is partial to the Democrats, especially Bill Clinton. The company has given Mr. Clinton's campaign more than $100,000. Its chairman, Robert Rubin, contributed $27,500 in soft (nonfederal account) money to the DNC and its congressional campaign committee. Rubin and his wife also gave $275,000 from their personal foundation (yes, foundations can give, too!) to the New York end of the Democratic National Committee.

His reward? He was named Secretary of the Treasury.

Most big corporations give to both parties, but some favor the Republicans, which they consider their natural home.

From 1991 through March 1996, according to the FEC, RJR Nabisco contributed $473,000 to the Democrats but almost twice as much—$847,000—to the Republicans. Philip Morris, Inc. was even more lopsided in its contributions; they gave $634,000 to the Democrats, but $2,174,000 to the Republicans.

Hollywood!

How about Hollywood? Well, traditionally they are in the Democratic camp, with gusto. Last time around, former Sony film chief Peter Guber gave $75,000 to the Democrats. The new DreamWorks chiefs are also generous. Jeffrey Katzenberg contributed $70,000, while David Geffen gave over $100,000.

In the 1995–96 giving cycle, Hollywood leaders kicked in again for the DNC's nonfederal accounts. According to the Federal Election Commission, big givers from L.A. include: Miramax Films, $100,000; David Geffen, $100,000; Sidney Sheinberg, then with Universal,

$100,000; Steven Spielberg, $100,000; and Lew Wasserman, also then with Universal, $100,000.

Rich individuals play an important role in keeping the parties afloat. Former President Bush had his own coterie of Republican wealthies. Called "Team 100," it was made up of those who contributed $100,000 or more.

The list—which actually numbered 249 millionaires—was topped by the omnipresent Dwayne Andreas, chairman of Archer-Daniels-Midland ("Supermarket to the World") who gave $1,071,000. A large contributor to Senator Dole and other breadbasket politicians, Andreas is no fool. In the Bush-Clinton contest he covered his usually large Republican wagers with a $270,000 contribution to the Democrats as well.

According to recent FEC reports from 1995, big givers include Joseph E. Seagram and Sons, $150,000 to each of the parties; Philip Morris, $600,000 to the Republicans; Revlon, $100,000 to the Democrats; Johnny Chung of California, $125,000 to the Democrats; Paine Webber, $100,000 to the Republicans; Deloitte & Touche accounting firm, $100,000 to the Democrats; Daniel S. Abraham of Palm Beach, $100,000 to the Democrats; $136,000 to the Democrats from Dr. Richard Gonzalez of Puerto Rico; and $140,000 to the Republicans from the American Financial Corporation of Cincinnati.

One wonderful sales pitch for the rich who love to press the flesh with the politically famous was a DNC sale on "Victory Train '92." For $25,000, you received three tickets to ride the train with party bigwigs from Washington's Union Station to New York for the presidential convention. The party promotional literature promised a nirvana for a political junkie.

"Once aboard, you'll be able to roam the train and enjoy the ride with Members of Congress, Democratic governors and mayors and DNC contributors from across the country," it said.

Lobbyists were welcomed, but journalists were barred. Investigative reporter Sheila Kaplan, however, managed to get aboard, and took photos of the lobbyists and elected officials laughing and enjoying the party on rails.

Choo-Choo Train

The Center for Public Integrity points out that the Republican 1992 convention in Houston was no better from a citizen's point of view. Corporations—including DuPont, Exxon, Shell Oil, AT&T—contributed $4 million (on top of the $11 million supplied by us taxpayers) for parties and galas. At a reception hosted by Atlantic Richfield (Arco), a small "Victory Train" chugged its way into the room. Waving from its caboose were none other than President Bush and Vice President Quayle! They had outdone the Democrats by bringing the train right into the convention hall.

There are numerous ways we can show our love for politicians, with the hope that it's not unrequited.

1. Individual "hard money" given directly to the candidate. One thousand dollars can be donated for the primary and another $1,000 for the general election, plus the same for spouse, and for each of the children.

2. $10,000 from each of the PACs, of whom the FEC says there were 4,016 at the beginning of 1996.
3. $20,000 in "soft money" from individuals to the party's "federal account."
4. *Unlimited amounts* from individuals to the nonfederal or state accounts of the parties.
5. *Unlimited amounts* by companies to the same nonfederal party accounts.
6. *Unlimited expenditures* by an individual on behalf of a candidate as long as it doesn't go through him or a party.

No. 6 highlights the irrational nature of campaign finance. It makes an end run around the system, showing that almost *everything* is possible under the ridiculous election law—if you know how to manipulate it.

An escape hatch of lobbying splendor is an exemption called "24E," or "individual expenditures." Unlike soft money, it can directly support a presidential candidate. And unlike the presidential candidate's own public-funded campaign, 24E has *absolutely no spending limit.*

There's a kind of Talmudic or metaphysical aspect to 24E. Although it can directly support a candidate, *it cannot do it with his input or any direct connection!* It's sort of like the three monkeys, or the "don't ask, don't tell" policy of Army homosexual screening transferred to the political world.

Willie Horton

Twenty-four E became famous in the 1988 Bush-Dukakis contest when Floyd Brown raised and spent a fortune on

Mr. Bush's behalf (supposedly without his knowledge or participation) by producing the Willie Horton television commercials that tried to show Mr. Dukakis as weak on crime. It featured the prisoner from Massachusetts, a parolee who helped sink Mr. Dukakis's chances for the Oval Office.

There is another gimmick (No. 7), which, like the IRS code in the hands of a brilliant CPA, makes the whole system fungible. This one is called "bundling." It's not a PAC because there is no pooling of funds. It's all individual gifts "bundled" together by a third party. No matter how filthy rich an individual is, if he wants to give directly to a candidate, the limit is $1,000 for the primary and $1,000 for the general election. (If he goes "soft," he loses the direct link with his favorite candidate, who may grant him a favor.)

But some smarty asked: Why not collect a slew of $1,000 contributions and "bundle" them into a hefty package which would otherwise be outlawed? Then the federal limit becomes meaningless and no one has broken the fatuous law.

Bundlers do just that, and the most successful is Emily's List. Who is Emily? Really no one. It is an acronym for "Early Money Is Like Yeast," and it is an organization based in Washington which only contributes to women candidates running on the Democratic ticket. As a PAC, which they also are, they can only contribute $10,000 to each candidate, $5,000 for the primary and $5,000 for the general election. But as bundlers, the sky's the limit.

Through the mail, they collect $100 minimum for

themselves, then an additional minimum of $100 each for two candidates—all the way up to the legal limit, which would be $4,000 per person, and $8,000 per couple, for two candidates. But speaking of end runs, if the donors chose, they could send in the $25,000 individual limit per person per election to Emily, to go to at least a dozen candidates, or as many as they wanted.

The checks are not made out to Emily's list. They are made out to individual Democratic women candidates recommended by Emily. The checks are then "bundled" up and sent to the candidate. When it comes to "legal" campaign finance gimmicks, no one is as ingenious as Americans.

How successful has Emily been since it began in 1985? Enormously. In the 1992 election year they raised $6.2 million through direct mail and gave an average of $100,000 to each of fifty-five women running for Congress. Twenty-five won.

In the FEC list of top fifty PACs (they are inaccurately listed that way) in 1993–94, Emily's List is No. 2, beaten out only by the Teamsters. In that election cycle, they sent an extraordinary $7,481,360 only to Democratic women, yet the total was almost as much money as the Teamster's fund, which went to hundreds of candidates in both parties.

Bundling as a Loophole

In 1994, though Emily raised a small fortune, many of their candidates were swamped in the Republican tsunami. Still, it's a very effective operation—if one likes "bundling."

Many don't. Emily calls its operation a "donor network," a pleasing euphemism for legally circumventing the law. But critics like Margaret Tabankin of the Hollywood Women's Political Committee disagree. "Bundling loopholes will undermine real campaign reform," she complains.

Institutionalized influence-buying mainly comes in the form of PACs. People can hardly believe it, but PACs started out as a "reform" in the post-Watergate era to stop the corruption of covert cash contributions. Now they're big business and tagged as the source of "special interest" targeting, perhaps the worst sin in influence peddling.

In the last election year, 1994, PACs took in $391,760,117, a mighty business that dispenses the money in an attempt to shape legislation to match their checks. The No.1 PAC is the Democratic Republican Independent Voter Education Committee, which is not a new party but the Teamster's fund.

The government workers' PAC, with over $6 million, is the No. 4 fund, organized to influence their bosses—the taxpayers—to continue their fattened existence. Other top PACs, which take in at least $3 million a year, include: the National Rifle Association ($6,831,000); the Trial Lawyers ($4,540,000); the National Education Association ($4,500,000; the teacher's union answered the phone in 1992: "Clinton and Gore"); the American Medical Association ($4,465,000); the United Auto Workers ($4,335,000); the Realtors' PAC ($3,554,000); the Machinists Union ($3,508,000); the Automobile Dealers Association (almost $3,000,000). One surprise: the United Parcel PAC was a hefty package of $2,854,000.

A PAC check in the mail (or better still, hand-delivered at a fund-raiser) is the easiest way to gain a politician's love. Without it, the onerous task of shaking a tin cup becomes even harder. PACs are the perfect tool for lobbyists, who make sure the money goes to the most cooperative congressmen, those attuned to their special interest goals.

The almost $400 million goes a long way. The average House member takes in some $275,000 of his campaign chest from PACs, more than half his budget. It's proportionately less in the case of senators, but still runs almost a $1 million per incumbent.

"I can't say that PACs are buying these elections," says former senator William Proxmire of Wisconsin (who refused to take PAC money or any other contribution), "but you'd have to be a fool to believe that they aren't buying something."

Of course, it's mainly the people in office who get the most PAC funds. (Power attracts money.) A study from the FEC shows that of PAC disbursements in 1994, some 72 percent went to incumbents, and 18 percent to open seats. *Poor challengers, the stepchildren of American politics, received only 10 percent of the PAC pool.*

Which politicians are the PAC champions?

Congressional Champs

In 1992, it was Democrat Dick Gephardt of Missouri, then the majority leader, who received $1,240,957 in PAC money. In the Senate, the winner was Republican Arlen Specter of Pennsylvania, who got $2,038,057 from PACs for his reelection bid.

In 1994, the cast changed a bit. Number one in the House was Speaker Tom Foley with $1,158,072, followed by fellow Dems Vic Fazio and Gephardt, with just over a million. Figures for the first half of 1995 showed Gephardt coming back into first place, just ahead of Newt Gingrich. (Power attracts money.)

Does PAC money buy influence and access?

You bet your sweet life it does. It not only focuses a member of Congress's attention on the PAC, but it diverts him away from his constituents, where his constitutional duties lie.

Former senator David Boren, who quit to become president of the University of Oklahoma, fears that's what too often takes place.

"Our constituents know what happens when there's someone who's able to control the flow of PAC money waiting to see us," he says. "And you have five minutes to see one person or another, and six to eight constituents are also competing for our time, and we're desperate to raise all that campaign money."

PACs come in all varieties, but the most esoteric, and perhaps the most dangerous, are the "Leadership PACs." In some strange convolution of the campaign law, politicians can own their own PACs, *but unlike the rule for other PACs, the sponsor can keep his name secret!*

What? Exactly. Take the PAC called "Campaign America." It's so large that it ranks as the No. 2 PAC in money disbursed, a significant $7 million in 1994. The money in these PACs doesn't usually go to its sponsor's campaign but is instead handed out in $10,000 parcels for political friends. It solidifies loyalty, helping the secret

PAC sponsor maintain power, especially in Congress. (The recipients know where the cash is coming from.)

Who owns Campaign America? Officially no one knows. Anyone named by the ghost politician can register it with the FEC—a friend, relative or any cover. And most important, they're sworn to secrecy. *But in a bureaucratic twist that defies logic, the Federal Elections Commission sends out a press release giving the rumored owners of the Leadership PACs!*

(It won't help to try to divine the logic behind this. There is none.)

"This is an UNOFFICIAL list," says the FEC bulletin. "The information is compiled by the FEC Press Office from media reports and not official agency records."

Top Secret

They go on to list seventy active secret Leadership committees, each with names fashioned from democratic (small "d") purple prose. In addition to Campaign America, there is the Effective Government Committee, whose undisclosed sponsor is reportedly Dick Gephardt, the House minority leader; New Republican Majority Fund (Republican Senate Whip Trent Lott); Committee for America's Future (Senator Robert Byrd); Victory USA (Vic Fazio, Democratic House whip); and of course GOPAC.

Virtually everyone in Washington knows that GOPAC is the piggy bank of Newt Gingrich. Who owns Campaign America? According to the FEC it had been Bob Dole, but as of September 1995 it was transferred to Dan Quayle.

The Leadership PACs imitate the smoke-filled backrooms in the era before primaries by allowing politicians to support other politicians—not at the will of donors but of the hand who doles out (excuse the expression) the money. Through Campaign America, for example, Dole-Quayle were able to disburse $1,674,104 in 1995 to 111 Republican candidates.

Their favorites, those who received approximately $10,000 each, were: Senators Judd Gregg of New Hampshire and Jesse Helms of North Carolina, and House members Spencer Bachus and William Zeliff.

The Democratic politician-to-politician fund handled by Democratic Leader Dick Gephardt, Effective America, took in $382,025 in 1995 and favored such people as House members Sam Gejdenson of Connecticut and Sander Levin of Michigan.

Web of Power

What's wrong with Leadership PACs, secret or not? It's that they're another strand in the Washington internal web, that bond between party politicians that ties them to Beltway mores, ideas and loyalties, instead of to their constituents. Obviously, they should be discontinued, as should all PACs.

Everyone knows that money is soiling the soul of American politics. But few seem to know what *really* must be done to fix it, permanently and effectively. I hope to be an exception.

The current fashion in reform, which is well-meaning, is to *somewhat* reduce the amount of money that's pumped into the system. It sounds good, but as we shall see, the apt comparison is like trying to reform the Mafia.

The best chance at a reform, which may pass the Congress in some form, is the bipartisan McCain-Feingold-Thompson Bill originating in the Senate, which has several backers in the House, including Chris Shays, Republican from Connecticut. John McCain, as most know, is the Vietnam War hero from Arizona, and a veteran conservative senator, while Russ Feingold is a relative newcomer from Wisconsin and a strong liberal. Fred Thompson, conservative Tennessee senator, is a former lawyer and Hollywood actor and one of the 1994 freshmen.

What is their plan?

The plan is not toothless, as is the recent Lobbying Disclosure Act of 1995 (see Chapter 7). It is well-meaning and should be encouraged, if only to show that it will eventually be proven *inadequate*, just as were the post-Watergate reforms. But to believe that it will clean up dirty American politics is naive, not unlike the well-nourished myth of the tooth fairy for children.

Some Good

The McCain-Feingold-Thompson Bill does a few good things: it will eliminate PACs—if the Supreme Court allows it, which is doubtful; it cuts down on the size of soft-money contributions; it cuts out most "bundling"; it requires that 60 percent of all monies be raised within the state where the candidate is running for election (in 1994, the Associated Press reported that Senator Joseph Lieberman of Connecticut had raised 85 percent of his money from out-of-state, mainly in California and Florida). It also bans incumbent use of franked—government paid—mass mailings in the year of an election and restricts the use of campaign funds for personal use, one of the great scams of our present system.

But what it *doesn't do* is drastically reduce the volume of money in the political world. The bill sets very high limits on what one can spend based on population. In California, $8.9 million is the proposed limit for candidates for the Senate, and in sparsely settled Wyoming, $1.5 million.

The problem? It's several fold. First, those amounts are about the same as—and in many cases exceed—those now being spent by candidates. And parallel bills discussed in the House have a $600,000 limit, which is *more* than is now spent on average! According to the Center for Responsive Politics, the average winner of a House race in 1994 took in $516,126.

In the Senate, the supposedly low Wyoming limit of the new proposal is considerably more than was spent in the senatorial race there in 1994, as is the amount actually spent in Hawaii and several other states. In that year, the average winner of a Senate contest spent $4,569,940, which is about the same amount they will spend under the new reform.

Too much money, and the television ads it buys, are chasing the voters. In the 1994 elections, all congressional candidates spent a total of $724 million. If this bill goes through, how much will be spent? The answer is simple: $724 million, or perhaps more!

Corrupting Cash

The volume of cash is what corrupts, whether it's in the Mafia, Hollywood, the U.S. Congress or the statehouse. People more clever than me or you will always find ways to appropriate and misuse it. And under the proposed reform, the amount of money is not going down. Nor will the number of distorted television commercials the money buys.

The second problem is that it's all voluntary. Candidates can just thumb their noses at the whole thing, and ignore the supposed inducements they will receive if they sign on.

What are the promised goodies?

1. A half hour of free prime-time television, paid for by the stations.
2. A 50 percent discount on paid television ads, also paid for by broadcasters.
3. Cheaper postal rates on two mailings per election.
4. Raising the $1,000 limit from individuals to $2,000 if the candidate's opponent doesn't sign on.

There are no matching funds as per the presidential races, and frankly, any politician worth his salt as a tin can shaker can do without the goodies. Instead, he'll continue to rely on raising an ever larger fistful of money for nasty television commercials that seem so effective. Or, if he's wealthy, he can ignore any new rules with imperious disdain.

The biggest problem, of course, is the Supreme Court. In a rather irrational decision in 1976 (*Buckley* vs.

Valeo), it equated spending money on campaigns with the First Amendment. They claimed that "money" equals "free speech," a rather dubious idea. Therefore, no one, not even Congress, could stop a candidate from spending any amount of money—either contributors' or his own—even if it went into the billions. It's as if the people have no control over their democratic process.

That court decision has made all reform iffy, which is why a true clean up of the system can only come with a comprehensive constitutional amendment that changes every precept of money in American politics.

Rich, Rich, Rich

Unlimited spending, especially for distorted television ads, is destroying the political process. In the case of wealthy candidates, it's not that they are worse, or more stupid, than other candidates. It's just that their swift intrusion of large amounts of cash disrupts other candidates who may be playing by the rules, as inadequate as they are.

We know that money does not assure victory. That was shown by the failed $28 million senatorial campaign of billionaire Michael Huffington in 1994. But as Steve Forbes did prove, it can catapult a man into the fray with much more force than those who are bound by rules.

Money can tilt the game enormously. Congressional incumbents, who outspend challengers almost three to one, for example, won 91 percent of the time in 1994, regardless of the Republican sweep.

Big change, not the incremental reform tried in 1974 and what's being proposed today, is the answer. To that end, we shall draft the 29th amendment to the Constitution (see Chapter 8), one which comprehensively changes the system of raising and spending money in American politics, and eliminates the multiple sins in one fell swoop.

Meanwhile, we shall continue to explain the extent of the Political Racket, showing why truly radical change is necessary if we are to escape the failures of Professional Politicians.

Corruption is one result, and it's there that we move next in our examination—the quid pro quo of cash for votes and favors, the ultimate shame of our system.

3

CORRUPTION IN THE RANKS

High Power and Low Morals

The FBI had heard that it was easy pickings.

Kentucky seemed to be one of those states where a clique of the favored in-crowd controlled the political process, and managed to cash in handsomely.

The state had a reputation for great racehorses, but with an enormous disparity between rich and poor, like Arkansas and Louisiana, it had a poor one for political integrity.

Was it deserved? It seems so.

In 1992, the FBI decided to initiate one of its sting operations against errant politicians, which had been so successful in the Abscam scandal of 1980. This one was called "Boptrot," and it began with the king of Kentucky lobbyists, John W. "Jay" Spurrier III. Spurrier was also a public official (a member of the state harness racing board), a convenient double play that's not unusual in certain regions of the country.

The lobbyist had arranged a bribe of $50,000 for a politician, in which he would financially participate.

Tipped to the arrangement, the FBI hid a transmitter in the briefcase that held the bribe money, and heard Spurrier exalt over the catch. He was offered leniency for his cooperation, which included his becoming a setup man for crooked politicians. The idea was to ensnare local politicians who took FBI-supplied cash after agreeing to pass legislation favorable to the harness track business. Simple quid pro quo, the legal basis of bribery.

The FBI outfitted Spurrier with a hotel suite in Frankfort, the state capital. Hidden video cameras photographed him as he dined, wined and bribed the friendly politicians who crossed his threshold with their palms up and outstretched.

The catch was enormous. Sixteen state legislators were convicted or pled guilty to various crimes, from fraud to extortion to bribery. The chief fish hooked was Speaker of the Kentucky House Don Blandford, who was caught taking a measly $500 bribe to kill a bill that would have hurt harness racing, a task he would gladly have undertaken without a fee.

"Bless your heart," he told the person who gave him the money as he stuffed the bait into his pocket.

Wages of Sin

Kentucky Speaker Blandford paid mightily for his petty theft—over five years in jail and an $108,000 fine. Also hooked was George Atkins, a former gubernatorial candidate and a lobbyist for Humana, a health care company. He promised a job to a woman legislator if she helped pass a bill for hospital expansion. The job never materialized, so Atkins just sent her $10,000. He had little choice but to plead guilty.

The Kentucky scam has had its positive result, as do many exposures of political corruption. It's a kind of cyclical motion—revelation and reform. It seems beneficial but there is no evidence that overall it has cut into political crimes.

In 1993, as a result of the exposé, the Kentucky legislature passed an ethics bill, which while not a model does slow down personal gain a notch. It limits lobbyists' wining and dining of lawmakers somewhat and keeps ex-legislators from entering their favored cash-in business—lobbying—for two years.

Corruption is rife in America, from the smallest communities to the West Wing of the White House, whichever party occupies it. Apparently, it's not only because the profession seems to attract an outsize proportion of the unethical, but because the stakes are very high.

All governments in America—federal, state and local—spend $2.7 trillion a year, 40 percent of the entire GDP, considerably more money than the Mafia ever dreamed of. There's enormous leeway in the decision as to who gets what portion of that enormous cornucopia. Naturally, both crooks and legitimate businessmen who want that tax exemption, that highway, that building permit, that government contract, *that everything*, will pay enormous sums to achieve their goals.

That's when politicians come into play. Their word, their encouragement, their bill, their committee staff influence, their friendly colleagues, can move millions (even billions) of dollars in one direction or another at the flick of a vote, or even an eyebrow. And they know it.

Among the ethical, it sets up a sense of enormous responsibility to do things fairly. Among the unethical, it's a chance for personal gain, especially cash.

Corruption at the Top

One of the most celebrated cases of corruption in high places involved a vice president of the United States, Spiro T. Agnew. Former governor of Maryland, he was elected VP on the Nixon ticket in 1968, then again in 1972, when they won the Oval Office over Democrat George McGovern in a landslide.

Agnew first rose to prominence as Baltimore county executive, then as governor of Maryland, where he came to Nixon's attention for his strong "law and order" stand in a time of civil unrest in the 1960s. Agnew was alleged to be on the take while county executive, when he ostensibly received $1,000 a week in kickbacks from contractors, architects and engineers, a practice which supposedly continued while he was governor.

The most startling aspect of the case was that Agnew's bribes allegedly still went on while he was vice president. It ostensibly began with a friendly $50,000 payment on his assuming the august office, with the understanding that he would help secure government contracts.

Agnew at first called the charges "damned lies." But after a federal grand jury began to hear the case, he quickly pleaded nolo contendere (no contest) to the charge of evading income tax on the tainted money, then resigned from office. According to U.S. Attorney James Thompson, the evidence for extortion was so strong that if the case had gone to trial, a conviction would have resulted. "The man is a crook," Thompson commented.

The most revealing fact of the case came out when Agnew told the court that in Maryland payments to politicians were so commonplace that companies simply budgeted for it!

Reflect on this. Agnew resigned in October 1973, just two months before the Watergate break-in. Had he not been caught in time, he would have ascended to become the thirty-eighth president of the United States when Nixon resigned in August 1974.

Corruption in high places is not unique. In April 1993, Governor Guy Hunt of Alabama went on trial before a jury in Montgomery, charged with having dipped into a nonprofit fund for his own use. Specifically, the money was in an inaugural kitty he had set up in 1987 to launch his second term as governor in style.

Take-Home Money

Hunt's fund-raising was so successful that, according to the prosecutor, there was a surplus of $200,000, which he allegedly diverted into his own bank account after the inauguration. It seems there had been an Alabama tradition of politicians personally appropriating excess campaign funds. In fact, the U.S. Congress had followed that infamous practice for years. Many congressmen who were retiring or defeated went home with a six-figure bankroll of someone else's money. Apparently, Hunt felt he was just following custom.

Even the Alabama ethics law was vague about that point, and friends of Hunt were saying it was just a good ol' boy technique. But presiding judge Randall Thomas ruled that dipping into excessive campaign funds "for direct personal gain" was illegal—something a schoolboy could have told him if the often shady political world wasn't involved.

After an eight-day trial, the jury found Hunt guilty. He surrendered his office five hours later, the fourth governor in American history to be convicted of a felony.

Washington, in both the legislative and executive branch, is a pulsating center for both unethical behavior and corruption. One of the most heinous was the HUD (Housing and Urban Development) scandal of the 1980s, which showed that the agency was riddled with influence peddling and special deals that cost the taxpayers multimillions of dollars.

An investigation by the House Committee on Government Operations issued a report on November 1990 that made the polemics of investigative journalists sound like a child's lullaby. Said the House report:

"During much of the 1980s, HUD was enveloped by influence peddling, favoritism, abuse, greed, fraud, embezzlement, and theft. In many housing programs, objective criteria gave way to political preference and cronyism, and favoritism supplanted fairness."

As the committee said, the rehabilitation program, "which was intended for the poor, became a cash cow which was milked by former HUD officials and the politically well-connected."

A HUD Transfer

The agency was rife with corruption. A HUD accountant, the House reported, "stole $1 million by electronically transferring the funds from HUD's account at Treasury to his personal account." Of course, that was only a minuscule portion of the fortune lost to taxpayers.

Samuel Pierce, the Secretary of HUD, came in for a scathing attack from the committee. "At best, Secretary Pierce was less than honest and misled the subcommittee about his involvement in abuses and favoritism in HUD funding decisions," the report stated. "At worst, Secretary Pierce knowingly lied and committed perjury during his testimony on May 25, 1989."

An independent counsel, Judge Arlin Adams, was appointed to investigate. He decided not to prosecute Secretary Pierce for many reasons, including Pierce's age and multiple health problems. But the former cabinet officer did sign a statement of apology that he had mismanaged the agency, which is an understatement.

In January 1996, new independent counsel Larry D. Thompson announced that the investigation was complete. The corruption had reached into high places in the federal executive suite. Former secretary of interior James G. Watt pleaded guilty to misinforming the grand jury investigation of HUD. In all, there were sixteen convictions of HUD officials and others, along with $2 million in criminal fines and the recovery of $10 million in extorted federal funds. Among those convicted in the HUD scam were the former treasurer of the United States, three former HUD assistant secretaries of housing and the executive assistant to the former HUD cabinet officer. Several of those convicted had to serve time in the federal pen.

Are the HUD scandals, the Kentucky legislative scam, the Agnew and Hunt cases just special incidents of political venality? Or is corruption rampant in America?

Are there perhaps fifty or so cases a year, aberrations in a generally moral environment? Are there a hundred cases a year? Surely not five hundred.

Try this: *The reality is that corruption by both elected politicians and government officials is epidemic.*

Criminal activity among members of Congress, for instance, far outweighs that of any other profession. Since 1970, thirty members of the House and Senate have been convicted of some type of criminal activity, ranging from racketeering to bribery to perjury to payroll padding to kickbacks to mail fraud to sex with minors to tax evasion.

Some House of Solons!

In 1978, Representative Joshua Eilberg of Pennsylvania pled guilty to illegally taking money for services in which the federal government had an interest.

In 1979, Representative Charles C. Diggs admitted inflating the salaries of his staff so they could kick back money to pay his personal expenses. Subsequently, he was convicted of mail fraud and making false statements to the government.

Also in 1979, Representative Frederick W. Richmond of New York pled guilty to tax evasion, illegally supplementing the salary of a federal employee and possession of marijuana. He resigned from Congress.

In 1980, Representative Daniel Flood of Pennsylvania was charged with the "use of official influence on behalf of private parties and foreign governments in return for unlawful payments." He resigned and pled guilty.

In 1984, House member George V. Hansen of Idaho was convicted of making false statements to the government, the first violation of the Ethics in Government Act. He had failed to report $200,000 in loans and income and was sentenced to five months in prison. His defenders argued that he had been singled out for harsher punishment while others had committed similar transgressions.

In 1987, Representative Mario Biaggi of New York was convicted of accepting illegal gratuities, conspiracy and obstruction of justice, and was sentenced to jail. Then in 1988, he was convicted of bribery involving a Bronx, New York, defense contractor and sentenced to eight years in jail. In 1991, he was released from jail because of failing health.

In 1988, Representative Patrick L. Swindall of Georgia was convicted on nine counts of perjury for lying to a grand jury about trying to negotiate a loan from a drug-money launderer despite knowing that part of the proceeds was derived from the sale of illegal narcotics. He was sentenced to a year in jail and disbarred.

In 1990, Representative Albert G. Bustamente of

Texas was convicted by a jury of accepting a $35,000 bribe from a food supplier for trying to get them a lucrative Air Force concession. His punishment? Three and a half years in jail and a substantial fine.

The Justice Department has established a Public Integrity Section, which tries to keep tabs on such crimes, or at least those prosecuted by federal authorities. Their latest "Report to Congress" (available to all citizens) is a wake-up call.

The annual total shows that 2,733 "Corrupt Public Officials," both elected and appointed, were convicted, indicted or awaiting trail during 1993 for crimes involving bribery, fraud, extortion or conflict-of-interest.

Since almost 3,000 public officials were actually caught in financial flagrante delicto, what should we assume? Probably that at least 10,000 such crimes are committed each year, a sad reflection on our body politic.

The Villains

The villains are greed and hubris. They stir up feelings among some politicians and officials that they are "special" people whose reward is the chance to exploit their office for privilege and benefits. That's not difficult considering the power we invest in our public officials. The difficult part for politicians is closing one's mind to personal gain, either for themselves or for friends, relatives and contributors.

But many can't resist the temptation, especially in the federal government, which won the 1994 corruption Olympics with 1,357 cases in one year.

The crimes range from venal bribery to padded

government expense accounts to illegal conflict-of-interest. James L. Emery, former administrator of the St. Lawrence Seaway and onetime minority leader of the New York Assembly, pled guilty to charging Uncle Sam $9,128.28 for personal travel costs, and received five years of probation.

They involve ingenious schemes to defraud, some petty, others significant. In Hawaii, Marvin Miura, director of the state's Office of Environmental Control, took better care of himself than the environment. He reccived $35,000 in bribes in exchange for awarding no-bid contracts to friends, and was sentenced to thirty-three months in prison.

Creative Voting

In Arkansas, there are a lot more violations than the twelve indictments handed down by the Whitewater prosecutor. Theortres Parham, a candidate for mayor of the town of Helena, was also deputy registrar for Phillips County, Arkansas, and had served on the Helena City Council. Knowing his way around—maybe too well—he decided to shortcut the election process by having voters sign blank applications for absentee ballots.

Dead men and women have long been voting in Chicago. Now Arkansas put a new wrinkle on the scam. Parham filled in the ballots of absentee voters with a vote for himself and returned them to the county clerk. He was sentenced to five months imprisonment for his creative scheme.

Sometimes, civil, not criminal, action is called for, especially in "influence" cases. Deputy Secretary of

Commerce Rockwell Schnabel received a call from his father-in-law, who was complaining that his company, which did business with the Veterans Administration, was suffering from delays in having their contract modified. Schnabel moved quickly into action. He personally contacted the deputy secretary of the VA. His request for quick action worked, but Schnabel paid a $5,000 civil fine for soliciting the favor.

(This case is particularly interesting because this type of lobbying is regularly done by congressmen and paid lobbyists, and under present law is absolutely legal. In fact—sadly—it's considered a job well done by lobbyists, and "constituent service" by congressmen. The rationale for punishing Schnabel is that it's not appropriate for federal officials. Obviously, it should be a general prohibition!)

Do the Justice Department lists show that political crime is decreasing or on the rise?

It seems to be a straight line upwards.

In 1974, the first year records were kept, there were a total of 523 cases convicted, indicted or awaiting trial. By the end of 1993, it had reached over 3,000.

What about geography? Which section of the country harbors the most crooked pols and bureaucrats?

Naturally, the Northern Illinois District, which covers Chicago (604 cases), and the Southern New York District, which covers the Big Apple (500), lead the pack. Others heavy in chicanery include Central California, which encompasses San Francisco (424), surprisingly far ahead of Southern California; and Eastern Pennsylvania (298). Southern Mississippi stands out with 111 cases for a lightly populated area, as does Northern Georgia with 188 cases.

Local Hijinks

Much political crime starts at the bottom, as it did with Agnew. Locally, the pickings are easy and conflict-of-interest laws are weak, even nonexistent. Local officials are bribed for such simple favors as zoning changes, assessments and city contracts. The economic gains for those who do the bribing are enormous. For a small investment, as little as a few hundred dollars, gains of millions can result. No wonder the practice is so widespread.

There are hundreds of ways for crooked politicians to play the put-cash-in-my-pocket game. In New York City, the tradition of graft was established in the nineteenth century with Tammany Hall, the crooked Democratic machine. It continued almost unabated, with the exception of the reform movement of Fusion candidate Fiorella La Guardia (the "Little Flower") in the 1930s, and hopefully again today with Mayor Rudy Giuliani, a former federal prosecutor in the mold of ex-DA Thomas E. Dewey.

Corruption in New York flourished in the postwar years, with new twists in the old scenario. In the 1980s, Donald Mannes, borough president of Queens, who was also the Democratic boss of that county (which if a city, would be the fourth largest in the nation), was implicated in an extortion-bribery scheme in the city's Parking Violations Bureau (PVB), where millions were missing.

He resigned his post, then committed suicide in the kitchen of his home by plunging a twelve-inch knife into his heart. The deputy director of the PVB, Geoffrey G. Lindenauer, admitted that he had extorted $410,000 in bribes from contractors and shared it with others, ostensibly including Mannes.

Friendly Jersey

New Jersey, just across the river from New York, has been under FBI investigation for some time, particularly because the state has had a reputation as the home of a profoundly powerful Mafia. Now the Justice Department is again looking into big-city political crime.

This time it's in what is commonly called "the inner city." Under U.S. Attorney Faith Hochberg, the Justice Department is conducting an investigation of corruption in Newark, the state's largest city. Thus far two former city council presidents have been implicated, along with the recent indictment of the chief of staff to Mayor Sharpe James, who is also a state assemblyman, on bribery charges.

Big-city Democratic machines have had a history of corruption, whether New York with Tammany Hall and Mayor Jimmy Walker, Boston under Mayor Curley and even Providence, Rhode Island, the "City on the Hill" founded by free-thinker Roger Williams, who fled the theocracy of the Massachusetts Bay Colony.

First controlled by old Yankees, leadership of the machine was ceded, over the years, to the Irish, then to the Italians, some with Mafia backing. Rhode Island became what many considered the most corrupt state in the Union.

As far back as 1905, muckraker Lincoln Steffens

wrote an article for *McClure's* entitled "Rhode Island: A State for Sale." (That dubious honor must now be ceded to Arkansas.) Observers believed that several of the state's politicians were in the pay of the Mafia, headed for many years by mobster Raymond L. S. Patriarca, informally known as "The Mayor of Providence." One wag asked: "How can you tell that the recession has hit Rhode Island?" The answer: "The Mafia had to lay off six judges."

By 1989, after Patriarca's son had taken over, twenty-one mobsters, including Junior, were convicted under the racketeering law (RICO). But the troubled state had its biggest shock coming on January 5, 1992, when corruption in Rhode Island came to a head in an explosive disaster. The once-apathetic population became furious.

Forty-five Rhode Island banks and credit unions were closed by the governor, tying up billions in depositors' money. The catastrophe hit one in three residents of the small state. The bank closings were triggered by a $15.9 million looting of the Heritage Loan and Investment Company by its proprietor, Joe Mollicone, Jr., a flashy businessman and friend of the Mob who drove both a Ferrari and a Mercedes.

Uncovered Banks

Just another S&L or bank fraud? Hardly. Many banks and credit unions in Rhode Island were not covered by the Federal Deposit Insurance Company (FDIC). Instead, they were self-insured by a state-regulated organization, the Rhode Island Share and Deposit Indemnity Corporation, or RISDIC. In fact, Mollicone was vice president of the group.

The problem was that RISDIC couldn't bail out depositors at the institutions because it had only $65 million to cover $1.3 *billion* in deposits.

Before the closings, Attorney General Arlene Violet, a former nun, issued a report which claimed that RISDIC was rife with fraud and that some credit union chiefs had made loans to themselves and each other. Violet went to the governor and asked for legislation to shift the insurance for the 300,000 depositors to the federal government. The bill was defeated by state legislators. Says Violet: "Federal insurance would have meant scrutiny they could never have survived."

The upshot of the bank disaster, according to a report in *Yankee* magazine, was a citizen revolt called "Right Now!" led by businessman A. G. Hassenfeld, the head of Hasbro, the toy makers. Before the revolt was over, Mollicone was in jail, a former governor was fined $30,000 for ethics violations, the mayor of one of the state's largest cities was convicted of racketeering, a state judge admitted to defrauding four banks and it was revealed that state legislators had approved over two hundred special pensions for friends and relatives—some of them dead or in prison.

Washington, however, refuses to be outdone in chicanery. One of the most sensational political indictments of our era involves the former chairman of the House Ways and Means Committee, Dan Rostenkowski. He was almost a caricature of power as he walked the halls of

Congress. According to government claims, he was also the epitome of political corruption.

A Friendly Congressman

A burly man who speaks in brusque Chicago shorthand, "Rosty," as he was known to those who both loved and feared him, was Chicago politics incarnate. He could have played himself in any movie of big-city bosses, even if transposed to Washington. Elected eighteen times (thirty-five years) by his working-class Chicago neighborhood, he operated in the tradition made famous by former mayor Richard Daley. Mike Royko in *Boss*, said that Daley had a moral code that went like this: "Thou shalt not steal, but thou shalt not blow the whistle on anybody who does."

Rosty, who had been a Daley lieutenant before coming to Congress, went one step further, say federal prosecutors. According to U.S. Attorney Eric Holder, noted for his work on political corruption, the former congressman dipped into the public trough to the tune of hundreds of thousands of dollars. Rostenkowski was so powerful in Washington over the past two decades that he virtually wrote and rewrote the IRS tax code several times. He had the power to grant exemptions and make changes worth millions to those favored by his imperial will.

He has since had his comeuppance. Rosty was defeated for Congress in 1994 in his working-class home district by a political amateur. A federal grand jury in Washington has indicted him on numerous charges including an excessive interest in the House Post Office, where he allegedly converted $21,000 in government stamps into cash for his large pockets. He is also charged with taking $28,000 in checks from his campaign donations and giving them to the post office, which allegedly converted them to cash and falsely reported the transaction as stamp purchases.

(If only such ingenuity had been applied to the federal budget, we'd long have dispensed with our $5 trillion debt!)

The veteran House postmaster, Robert V. Rota, has pleaded guilty in the cash for stamps scheme.

Long Indictment

Rostenkowski's indictment, which covers seventeen points, also charges that he allegedly had a crowd of fourteen workers who did little or no work for the government, but took in a total of $500,000 in federal salary over a period of twenty-one years, while they actually did personal work for Rostenkowski and his family, including cutting the grass. In at least one case, the indictment alleges the worker was asked to turn some of the money back to the congressman.

According to the government, Rosty was a gracious and free spender, buying gifts for others in the House stationery store with his congressional office funds.

A federal appeals court reviewed the indictment prior to trial, and advised the lower court that six of the indictment points might not be reasonable, and should be reviewed.

In March, 1996, the federal district court threw out four of those six counts—those involving lying to Congress (apparently it is not a crime for a member of

Congress to lie to Congress!) but kept in those involving theft. In April 1996, Rostenkowski pleaded guilty to two counts of mail fraud. He will go to jail for seventeen months and pay a $100,000 fine.

Is any of this new, or are we just catching more errant politicians?

It's hard to say, but things surely were not spanking clean in the world's first great democracy, although corruption was not at the present level. Problems ranging from conflict-of-interest to bribery arose in George Washington's administration.

Revolutionary Tales

Secretary of War Henry Knox entertained beyond his means and his wife's gambling debts crippled him. In 1791, Knox tried land speculation in Maine, which led to a series of lawsuits. To bail himself out, he recommended friends for public office, who in turn helped him with his debts and legal problems—pure influence peddling and an indirect form of bribery.

Washington had to dismiss several collectors of the Treasury for indiscretions in their handling of funds. Under President John Quincy Adams, Dr. Tobias Watkins, a high-ranking officeholder, was tried for embezzlement, then imprisoned by the next president, Andrew Jackson.

Corruption flourished in the Civil War as fortunes were made by suppliers who often bribed public officials to get lucrative contracts. It led to the dismissal of Secretary of War Simon Cameron and the passage of the first set of conflict-of-interest laws. Criminal penalties were instituted for violation of what had previously been considered mere ethical questions.

(The fine line between the two—ethics and criminality—is still heavily debated, as we shall see in Chapter 6.)

The administration of General U. S. Grant, the great Civil War hero, has been considered the most corrupt in history. Much of his staff, even his family, were involved in financial misconduct, but prosecutors never tied it directly to Grant himself, who died poor.

After that, the emphasis of political crooks mainly shifted from the outright stealing of money, to the use of the power to *influence* events, with payment in return. This "influence peddling," sometimes called "honest graft," was best exploited by such political bosses as George Washington Plunkitt of Tammany Hall, a powerful exponent of the art.

Politicians still took kickbacks from suppliers, but they also extended their reach by using inside information—like where a new road was going to be built—to buy the land cheaply for later resale to the city.

The Spouse Racket

Expensive gifts to politicians were quite commonplace. In 1890, Grover Cleveland's wealthy postmaster, John Wanamaker, presented Mrs. Cleveland with a seaside home on Cape May, New Jersey. When it became public, Cleveland hurriedly sent Wanamaker a check for $10,000.

This system of offering gifts to the woman of the family instead of to the politician himself—what might be called the "spouse racket"—was popular. Apparently it still is, although not as easily accepted by the public. Hillary Clinton's receipt of what many consider a gift of $100,000 in commodity future profits and the resulting media attention is proof that the public no longer approves of this backdoor method.

Gifts are now banned in the executive branch, which has gotten some staffers in grave difficulty. One famous example was the vicuña coat gift to Eisenhower's chief of staff, Sherman Adams, the former governor of New Hampshire. That resulted in Adams's dismissal after a noteworthy career.

But the public has been more lenient about gifts to presidents themselves, at least once they had left office. For example, President Eisenhower received $40,000 in gifts from wealthy admirers for his retirement home in Gettysburg, Pennsylvania.

Ike, for one, didn't apologize for a minute. As a senior staffer noted, "The Office of the President is too big to be influenced by any gift." Perhaps it was true then, but the Watergate-Whitewater events have traumatized much of the public. And besides, our former presidents are now treated like royalty with taxpayer funds, probably to avoid such conflicts.

The American public, finally, is in a heated reform mood and desperately wants cleaner government. There is a heightened awareness to match the declining morality of American politics and the billions raised and spent in campaigns. The mood is one which should be capitalized on immediately if we are to turn the tide.

That may be why the public tolerates, even applauds, the entrapment method used in FBI "stings" which finds, indicts and convicts many of the political errant, as in the Kentucky case.

Is it fair for the FBI to create political criminals by enticing them with bribes?

Hard to say, except that the theory is that many politicians are probably committing bribery and extortion anyway, and this is a simple way to expose them. The argument continues, but meanwhile the FBI has completed several sting operations against politicians, and has an undisclosed number still going on.

An Early Sting

The first large-scale political sting was the well-known Abscam, which took place in the late 1970s and snared a passel of pols. Word was passed around Washington that Arab sheiks were coming to town with unlimited funds to spread around. Actually, of course, the "Arabs" were FBI agents dressed up for the kill.

Renting a Washington town house, a luxurious Florida home, an elegant yacht and New York hotel rooms, the fake Arabs told the politicians who flocked to them that they needed help in making investments, getting casino gambling licenses and influencing the immigration service to allow fellow Arabs to enter the country. The locations were spiked with secret videotape and recording devices.

When it was all done, the FBI net had snared thirty-one public officials, including seven members of Congress, who were indicted for bribery and conspiracy. The matchmaker in many of the deals was Mayor Angelo J.

Errichetti of Camden, New Jersey, who was convicted for his efforts.

Congressman Michael O. Myers of Pennsylvania was shown taking $50,000 and was expelled from the House, the first such case since 1861. Several of the congressmen pleaded "entrapment," but all were found guilty on some charge. Congressman John M. Murphy of New York was acquitted of bribery but found guilty of accepting an "unlawful gratuity," a lesser charge. Congressman Richard Kelly of Florida admitted taking $25,000 (he told Arabs that "If I told you how poor I am, you would cry") but claimed it was part of his own investigation of corruption. Kelly was initially convicted, but that decision was later overturned by the courts.

The most important snare was twenty-three-year veteran of the U.S. Senate Harrison Williams. After a distinguished career, Williams had succumbed to greed and had agreed to help the fake Arabs obtain a federal contract to build a titanium mine in Virginia. He was to receive $12.5 million, perhaps the largest bribe in political history. Sentenced to prison, Williams quit the Senate before he could be expelled.

Another Sting

The sting method has been so successful that the Justice Department and the FBI used it not long ago in Sacramento, California, to settle a philosophical argument involving reward for favors, the legal basis of bribery.

But surely bribery has nothing to do with your typical politician. He wouldn't think of taking cash for himself. Right? But he would take a campaign contribution, perhaps with the understanding that down the line he'd be doing a favor for the large contributor, even if it wasn't spelled out.

Isn't that the way the whole system works? Isn't that why a corporation will give a great deal of money to both parties—to protect some tax break or federal handout or ecological rule they need? That surely isn't criminal.

Don't be so sure about that.

Even without the bribe in the pocket, there may be the wink or the confidential handshake. We've always assumed that as long as a politician didn't directly take money for his own pocket, and though he might be guilty of unethical thoughts (so what's new?), at least he wasn't really a criminal.

Now a handful of prosecutors are asking the courts to stretch the definition of bribery and extortion, right into the world of campaign finance. They are not blindly accepting what is considered "normal" and "usual" in the raising of money. What used to be considered just a little shady or bordering on unethical in fund-raising may now be seen as criminal.

If the vote of the politician, or even his influence, was exchanged for an otherwise legal campaign contribution, it could be considered quid pro quo, and therefore a crime. (In Latin, it translates as "something for something," but in the American vernacular, it's perhaps best expressed as "you scratch my back and I'll scratch yours.")

That's a frightening thought that should make all politicians shudder.

It came into play in Sacramento, California, not long

ago when federal prosecutors decided to use the now-classic sting to snare state legislators around whom rumors of impropriety were flying.

George L. O'Connell, who was U.S. attorney in Sacramento from 1991 to 1993, and an assistant attorney in the 1980s, decided to take on unethical legislators. He received a tip from a lobbyist that certain politicians in the California State Legislature had their hands out, hinting there could be action for the right campaign contributions.

O'Connell "wired" the lobbyist to record his conversations with the suspect legislators. To make the sting work, he even set up a fake company, GULFSHRIMP, which pretended it was opening a processing plant in California.

"The lobbyist who was wired," relates O'Connell, "told the legislators about the project and asked for their support, including the passing of a private bill to help GULFSHRIMP. In return, the legislators asked him: 'How helpful will you be?' referring to campaign contributions. The lobbyist offered the legislators contributions if they worked with him, and they accepted the FBI-supplied money, along with honoraria fees for making speeches. This involved sizable money—more than $20,000 in campaign contributions and several thousand for each breakfast appearance."

Implicit Clues

O'Connell points out that even though the politicians did not *explicitly* agree to pass the bill in exchange for contributions, they did make it clear in the recordings that

that was what they intended—a vote for campaign money.

He prosecuted on three statutes: the RICO, or racketeering act; the charge of Extortion Under the Color of Official Right; and of accepting Illegal Gratuities. When the sting was completed, five sitting California state legislators were convicted and received prison sentences from eighteen to thirty-three months. Also convicted were three legislative aides, one state commissioner and two lobbyists. The courts have since upheld the convictions.

Stanley M. Brand, a Washington defense attorney who handles many corruption cases, is worried that the prosecutors are going too far.

"If it continues," he warns, "campaign contributions will come to mean campaign bribes. I'm afraid that the D.C. Circuit Court's decision on the campaign contribution cases is wrong. They have expanded the statutes excessively."

Brand was talking about a decision that makes it unnecessary for a prosecutor to show *exact* quid pro quo to convict a politician for bribery. All they need prove is that he agreed to take a campaign contribution, or received one after the fact—an "illegal gratuity"—while knowing that he intended to respond with a vote or a favor.

Said the Court: "No politician who knows the identity and business intent of his campaign contribution is ever devoid of knowledge as to the inspiration behind the donation."

In effect, the Court was saying: "Who are you kidding, Congressman? Better beware! If you take a contribution and you think the giver expects some legislative action in return, then you don't have to assure him of anything in advance, and you still might be acting in a criminal way. And besides, we don't have to prove it exactly!"

Public Action

When will it all end? When can we expect our public officials to act at least as well as ordinary citizens so we don't have to entrap them in a sting?

Whatever the courts eventually do, the public must act to change the entire system. To envision a complete end to political corruption, whatever we do, is naive. But neither should we yield to the cynicism that the bleeding can't be stemmed by public pressure.

The biggest obstacle is the POLITICAL ESTABLISHMENT, which makes the rules that encourage corruption—both in its laxity of oversight and its insistence that political campaigns be financed like small wars.

If not ended, can it be cut way back?

Absolutely. I have developed a plan which will hopefully change the behavior of our public officials, mainly through totally reforming the political landscape. I will detail that along with other suggested reforms, some quite radical, later in this work.

Corruption operates individually in most cases. But it's part and parcel of the present two-party system in which it flourishes. Without that antiquated operation, politicians might act less self-serving and more like regular citizens, and with more concern for the public than they exhibit.

Now, let's look at the two big parties which dominate us. Let's see if they're performing responsibly or if they've set the stage for continued lack of ethics, the Achilles' heel of democracy.

4

THE TWO PARTY MACHINES

"Now Is the Time for All Good Men *Not* to . . ."

Every nation develops a unique system for choosing its leaders.

There have been tribal chieftains and hereditary kings and queens. In Tibet, for thousands of years, the senior monks chose an alert small boy, supposedly a spiritual reincarnation, to become the Dalai Lama. In ancient China, a series of nationwide examinations chose the brightest young philosophers to become the Mandarin rulers under the emperor.

In Plato's *Republic*, future leaders would be supported by the state and raised in a Utopian atmosphere to protect them from the ravages of connivance and corruption in which traditional politics are steeped.

And in America? How do we choose our leaders?

We have Iowa and New Hampshire, two early vote crushing affairs that are often unrepresentative of the national will.

The primary system began in 1901 with progressive reformer Bob La Follett in Wisconsin. Oregon and two other states joined in 1901, and other states adopted primaries over the years. But party bosses still chose the nominee until 1952, when the New Hampshire primary picked Dwight Eisenhower over Robert Taft. Today, some three-fourths of the states hold public primaries, each with their own set of rules.

In February 1996, after trudging through Midwest cornfields and the icy roads of New England, nine Republican presidential hopefuls faced the voters in surely the most idiotic method of choosing national leaders ever invented in a free society.

The prize in the two primary contests was forty-one delegates to the Republican National Convention in San Diego, representing just 2 percent of the 1980 delegates who would choose the party's nominee for president.

To obtain this handful of delegates, the wannabes had spent some $40 million. In Iowa alone, they expended $10 million to attract the 100,000 (only one in six Republicans) who came out to caucuses in schools and basement dens. Counting the monies spent leading up to Iowa, the tally came to about $200 a vote, enough to make old Boss Tweed disgusted with the inefficiency of modern vote buying.

What's worse is that the whole Iowa experience was

a farce. Five of the nine Republican presidential candidates were effectively finished after this minuscule test of voter sentiment. But what the American people were not told was that not a single Iowa delegate to the national convention was chosen that night! A state convention held later on chooses its twenty-five delegates regardless of the caucus votes.

False Drama

With few exceptions, journalists tried to falsely heighten the drama by not telling the American public the truth, if they even knew it. In reality, the Iowa caucus was just another of the meaningless, poorly attended "beauty contests" run by several states.

(Phil Gramm was snookered into believing his party's own propaganda and dropped out after Iowa.)

New Hampshire was a true primary, but with an Alice-in-Wonderland, even childish, twist. One of the smallest states in the Union, with only a little over a million residents (about half the size of the Bronx), its vanity as the "first primary state" has given it undue, undeserved and ridiculous prominance.

The Crazy Quilt

The presidential primary system is a crazy quilt that makes it impossible to properly evaluate the results. Across the land there are a variety of eligibility rules that are uncoordinated with other states. In several, like California, only Republicans can vote in the Republican primary. In others, including New Hampshire, both Republicans and Independents can vote. In some, including

Wisconsin, there are "open primaries," a strange phenomenon in which everyone, even opposition Democrats, can intrude in the Republican primary, and vice versa.

What that does, of course, is muddy the waters. Why not, the Dems might say, help pick the weakest Republican nominee?

The way the delegates are awarded often makes little sense. New Hampshire divides the vote into a proportionate number of delegates for each candidate who gets 10 percent of the vote or more. But big California, with 165 delegates, the largest crop at the Republican National Convention, gives *all* of them to the top person in the primary race—winner take all.

That's the banal rule in many states. Check out the failure of logic in the example of California, the eight-hundred-pound gorilla of American politics. There are 5.3 million Republicans in California. About 40 percent, or 2 million, vote in the presidential primary. If, for example, the top candidate gets 25 percent, or 500,000 votes (one in ten Republicans) and the next candidate gets 24 percent, the "winner" walks away with all 165 delegates.

The second-place candidate, who lost by one percent, or 5,000 votes, doesn't even get a booby prize. There is no runoff, just regrets, to both the loser and democracy.

It's absolute nonsense. Like the entire presidential primary system, it is a fantasy the two parties have created to please themselves, and have passed off as a service to the public.

And now—jealous at New Hampshire's pride in being first—other states have frenetically moved up their presidential primary dates. Delaware has shifted uncomfortably close to New Hampshire by holding its primary four days later, on February 24. New York, which used to hold its primary in April, now votes just two weeks after Delaware, on March 7. California, whose primaries were generally just a footnote to history in June, now votes on March 26. (In response, an angry New Hampshire pressured most of the main candidates to ignore Delaware as a primary interloper!)

By April 1, almost three-fourths of the 1996 Republican delegates were named. Despite the elaborate folderol preceding New Hampshire, the nominating process now goes very quickly afterwards.

National Primary

What should we do instead of our present inadequate primary system?

The answer is quite simple. We need a national party presidential primary in which the party voters will directly chose their nominee across the land on the very same day.

If the parties did not cooperate in instituting it or a similar system, it might require legislation, or even a constitutional amendment, to put it into effect. Since we no longer nominate our candidates in smoke-filled rooms, we need to have a uniform primary system. It should work something like this:

1. Only people registered in that party shall be able to vote. There will be no "open" or "crossover" primaries.

2. There will be no caucuses or delegates chosen by state conventions, nor will there be any delegates chosen by state primaries.
3. There shall be a series of two national primary elections, each held on the same day throughout the country. In the first, held in March, *all* party candidates will compete.
4. If no one receives a majority of the votes, there will be a second election in June in which only the top two vote-getters will participate.
5. The candidate who receives a majority of the votes will become the party's nominee for president.
6. A national convention shall be held in July to confirm the nominee and adopt a party platform.

This will make the choice clear. The winner will have a majority and there will be no more strange, state-by-state aberrations.

Who engineered the present ineffectual and confused primary system? Obviously, the two political parties of Republicans and Democrats—who have cleverly convinced the nation that they are a shadow government which must be obeyed.

The primary and general election systems developed by them, with the connivance of the state legislatures they control, have made elections in this country a tightly controlled operation.

Presidents, congressmen, governors and others are often elected without a majority. Independents are easily frozen out. Campaign finance laws are written to maintain the hegemony of the two parties. Ordinary citizens who are not millionaires dare not run for office unless they first join a party's inner circle.

Why do we have parties to begin with? They are only private organizations. In Washington, the Democrats are incorporated as the DNC Services Corporation and the Republican National Committee is a nonprofit group. We have traditionally, and apparently smilingly, turned our democracy over to them.

Why?

Partyless Founding

People assume that political parties were an inherent part of our founding. Quite the opposite. The nation began with the optimistic thought that it could be a "Republic of Virtue," unencumbered with political parties and self-interest.

George Washington expressed it best at his Farewell Address at Fraunces Tavern in downtown New York when he showed himself to be more of a prophet than he's given credit for. He referred to parties sneeringly as "factions," and warned "of the baneful effects of party." He feared that partisanship would rip apart the emotions of the American people and injure the nation, a telling comment on politics today.

John Taylor shared the same fears. In a letter to John Adams, he said: "All parties degenerate into aristocracies of interest," warning that the public had to watch out for where "integrity ends and fraud begins" within the parties.

Initially, Washington's way worked. At the Electoral College of 1788, he was elected president by unanimous vote. But it wasn't long before his second term was over in 1796 that the obvious differences in ideology gave birth to our political parties.

There were other reasons besides ideology. It was an era of poor communications and transportation, and many believed that these clubs were necessary engines of the political process. People of like mind, isolated from each other—from New Hampshire to Georgia—needed a mechanism to mobilize the voters countywide, statewide and nationally. Segments of the population chose up sides, and though they might not agree on all issues, felt a common bondship.

Education on the issues of the day was difficult. Party leaders provided the direction and chose the nominees almost without citizen participation. It was indirect democracy, the hallmark of our whole system until recently.

The original parties were amorphous but, like the two major ones today, had views that were diametrically opposed. It began right in Washington's cabinet, where Alexander Hamilton argued for a strong central government and on behalf of wealthier citizens, whom he believed added to the nation's stability.

Jefferson's Thesis

Secretary of State Thomas Jefferson believed otherwise—that a decentralized, smaller government where ordinary farmers and tradesmen could be truly free from government control was the proper route for democracy to strengthen. In speaking of taxes and government, both of which he felt should be kept at a minimum, he said:

"[A] wise and frugal government, which shall restrain men from injuring one another, which shall leave them otherwise free to regulate their own pursuits of industry and improvement, and shall not take from the mouth of labor the bread it has earned. This is the sum of good government. . . ."

Out of these two opposing views grew the first two parties: the Federalists of Hamilton (who was killed in a duel by Aaron Burr) and John Adams, Washington's vice president, and the Anti-Federalists, led by Jefferson and Madison.

(It is ironic that today, the roles of the parties have been virtually reversed. Jefferson, who is a hero of the Democrats, would have been outraged by the Washington-run mammoth government that takes the lion's share of the people's income. And the Democrats, who traditionally despise Hamilton, are enthusiastically following his theory of large, centralized government.)

The Jeffersonian party soon became the "Democratic-Republican" party, but generally used the name "Republican" to identify more with the French Revolution than the British monarchy. They sought to extend populism, and the rights of the mass of the people, as long as it wasn't under central control.

The Federalists soon died out for two reasons: they were pro-British and thus on the wrong side of the War of 1812, and they stressed their interest in the well-to-do over the masses of voters. The Republican-Democrats won the five elections from 1800 on, putting Jefferson, Madison and Monroe in the White House, the so-called Virginia Dynasty.

By 1824, the party picture was clouded. The Republican-Democrats were naming their presidential candidates out of public view, in caucuses of congressmen. The revolt against party control resulted in four candidates for president, three of whom were put up by state legislatures and petition. The "endorsed" candidate, Henry Clay, came in last. This was a real revolution.

The present Democratic Party started in 1828 with the election of Andy Jackson as president, and his fight against privilege and monopoly. He also set up the "spoils" system, which awarded enormous patronage to the winning party, a system that still exists.

The Whigs

To fight Jackson, the former Hamiltonians and Federalists organized the Whig Party, which brought back two-party government (Whigs against the Democrats) and elected such people as Henry Clay and Daniel Webster to Congress, along with two presidents, William Henry Harrison and Zachary Taylor, both former military men. But the Whigs were not up to handling the antislavery fight that began in the 1850s. The Democrats were pro-slavery, and although the Whigs fought against its extension into the West, they were not vigorous enough.

One former Whig congressman from Illinois, Abe Lincoln, joined the new Republican Party, which was a national third party formed in 1854.

The Republicans were a pro-business, pro-Union, pro-expansionist party. They lost their first presidential election in 1856 under the banner of John C. Frémont, hero of the Indian wars. But by 1860, they had taken the White House with Lincoln winning in a four-way race.

Thus, the present two parties, the Republicans and Democrats, were firmly established and have ruled for 135 years, uninterrupted, sharing the Oval Office and the Congress.

And today? What of the two major parties?

We have already seen the record of campaign finance corruption, and of actual criminality in their ranks. And now we've seen their disruptive national primary system and iron-fisted methods of keeping the interlopers (read "people") out of their affairs through connivance. Is their record, both in ruling the nation and in their advocacy of better democracy good, fair or rotten? Arc there other ways in which we can enhance the people's voice in the present system?

Yes, there are many. We shall look at a few now, and then later examine what can be done to invite more Americans into the political process and reduce the power of these two giants. In fact, unless the system can be altered to curb their self-interest, we might even entertain the notion of eliminating them entirely.

With perfect citizen communication and daily education on the candidates and issues, these political parties—as I shall try to show—may be more of a hindrance to democracy than an asset.

A Connecticut Sampler

Let's take a look at one of our oldest states, Connecticut (which happens to be my home), and see how the parties manipulate the public to achieve their narrow self-interest.

Connecticut has a unique twist on presidential primaries. You don't even have to apply to run. They use the media as a criteria! Says the law: "Each person whose candidacy for that party's nomination is generally and seriously advocated" in the media is automatically put on the ballot. If you want to get your name *off*, you have to apply to the Connecticut secretary of state.

Connecticut used to apportion delegates according to the primary vote, but it has now joined the yahoos in "winner take all," the backward trend that is plaguing the nation. Why? Because politicians don't want a split delegation, preferring instead to disenfranchise the voters.

In some ways, Connecticut, the nation's first democracy, is now one of the least democratic (small "d") states in the Union. Founded in 1639 when Thomas Hooker left the theocratic Massachusetts Bay Colony to establish nearby Connecticut, the colony was truly a departure. No longer was there a religious test for voting, and it became the first government to establish near-universal suffrage for adult men. It's "Fundamental Orders," the first written constitution, earned the state the sobriquet (right on its license plates) of "The Constitution State."

That's historically accurate, but the state has turned its back on its glorious heritage. Its two major parties use every trick in the politician's handbook to deny modern democracy to its voters. In forty-seven states, for instance, people who want to run for office—from state legislator to governor to senator to congressman—can enter a "direct" primary and have the *voters* choose the party nominee.

But not in backward Connecticut. There, politicos decide for the voters, just as in the old Tammany Hall days of New York.

Instead of direct primaries, the Connecticut Republican and Democratic Parties meet in local conventions and "endorse" their candidates for state legislators and members of the U.S. House. For statewide offices, from governor to U.S. senator, the delegates choose their nominees at a state party convention. If someone wants to contest that choice and go "public," he must receive the backing of 15 percent of the delegates, and then run a challenge primary.

It's not only an uphill battle, it's also too late to be effective. That primary is held on September 10, less than two months before the general election, putting the nominee—even if he should win the challenge primary—behind the eight ball in the general election.

Major and Minor

Connecticut politicians in both parties have created a clever, convoluted system to frustrate the public will. The state has no Initiative or Referendum law, blocking the people's voice on legislation. It has no recall law to kick out any elected officials with whom the public is disgusted. It has set up an ingenious system of "major" and "minor" parties in order to thwart the creation of strong independent parties. It even permits—in fact, authorizes—false local elections that are patently unconstitutional, as we shall see.

It seems to specialize in elected officials who do not get a majority of the voters. Former governor Lowell Weicker was elected with only 40 percent of the vote, while the current governor, John Rowland, received only 37 percent. That's not the fault of the candidates, but they do nothing about it once in office.

The reason these governors can win without a majority is that there is no runoff, a second election to decide the true choice of the people. The lack of runoffs is an antidemocratic tradition in almost all of America. Only Georgia requires a majority to elect members of Congress.

The Connecticut distinction of "major" and "minor" party is another gimmick that cleverly kills any chance of true opposition to the two-party monopoly. If a party receives 20 percent of the vote in the last gubernatorial election, they can automatically place all their candidates on the state ballot, from governor down to mayor.

But if you are designated a "minor" party, you must qualify each office separately, an excessive burden for a new or small party trying to challenge the giants.

Simple proof that politicians *actively* discriminate against independent and third parties is written right into the Connecticut law. The state pays for and administers primaries only for the top two parties in the state. All other parties must fend for themselves!

The state also has a law called "minority representation," which is an absolute political travesty. It has nothing to do with race or ethnicity. It just protects the two major parties, probably unconstitutionally, in local elections, where it permits unopposed totalitarian-style elections in which the candidates are generally *unopposed.*

Gimmicky Election

In Greenwich, Connecticut, for example, the Board of Estimate and Taxation, which sets the budget and tax rate, has twelve members who are all elected in the same year. In reality, those elections are fake, just a gimmick to please the two major parties.

In a strange reversal of American tradition, each party puts up a maximum of six candidates, or a total of twelve from the Democratic and Republican Parties—who now assume the ex officio role of governments.

The trick is simple: *Voters are only allowed to vote for six of the twelve candidates*, which means there is usually no contest. All twelve Democrats and Republicans are elected, even if some of them receive only one vote. There is no opposition unless a third party tries to beat the system, which has happened without success. People assume that since the Donkey and the Elephant are recognized as controllers of the Board, there *must* be something legitimate about the system.

The funny side effect is that the Democrats, who are only 20 percent of the Greenwich electorate, automatically get 50 percent of the board. One tragic aspect is that there are just about as many "Unaffiliated" voters in the state of Connecticut as Republicans, but they are totally left out from picking up seats in this and other blatant voter frauds. No wonder Americans increasingly do not trust the major parties.

(In Greenwich and other places in the state, the Board of Education is also chosen in this same method, which may explain the steady erosion in student scholarship.)

When confronted with the obvious lack of democracy, Connecticut politicians exclaim: "But it works!" Of course, but so did Mussolini's train schedules.

What about the courts? Won't they overturn such undemocratic laws?

The Connecticut courts have heard challenges but have upheld the law, which is an obvious violation of the Fourteenth Amendment and the principle of one-man, one-vote. But remember: Judges receive their judgeships because of their party affiliations, not because they are unbiased citizens.

Exploiting Apathy

To most Americans, politics is the exclusive province of politicians, which, of course, is the secret to the power of the professionals. Their genius is the ability to exploit the apathy and fears of the American voter at every level of government.

In New York State, there is a direct primary, but politicos have it rigged so that the "endorsed" candidate of the party is almost sure to win the primary. How do they do that? Simply by conniving to make sure that no one else gets on the ballot statewide.

In the March 1996 presidential primary, for example, Bob Dole was the official candidate of the party, and a sure winner because of the petition rules. In order to get on the ballot statewide, a candidate needed 1,250 signatures or 5 percent of all registered Republicans in each of the state's thirty-one congressional districts.

Sound possible? Perhaps, but not if the "official" party is frantically signing up most Republicans for its candidate, and uses every technicality to challenge opposition signatures. For example, if someone leaves off his middle initial, that name is voided. One state politician estimated that only 30 percent of the names ever make it through the Board of Elections screening process.

It's bossism at its worst, a common fact at the local and state levels. No wonder Dole's opponents had trouble even getting on the ballot. In one, Buchanan collected more than enough—1,626 signatures—but the Dole-controlled Board of Elections ruled 480 signatures invalid, knocking Buchanan out. Lamar Alexander declined to even appear on the New York ballot, knowing that spotty representation would make him look weak. It took a lawsuit by Steve Forbes and the intervention of the courts to get solid opposition to Senator Dole on the ballot.

Party power is used regularly, especially to thwart third parties who might knock them off their perch.

Keeping the People Away

The technique is simple: just regularly increase the number of signatures needed for a new party to get on the state ballot. The "Ballot Access News" has developed a chart to show that continuous, insidious move by state legislatures of both parties. In all there have been thirty-seven drastic *increases* in the number of signatures required. In 1983, North Carolina jumped from an attainable 5,000 all the way up to 36,949. In 1995, Alabama tripled their requirement. In 1980, Indiana increased it fivefold, from 7,000 to 35,000.

Massachusetts at one time required only 1,000 signatures to get on a statewide ballot, but the legislature, fearful of competition from a third party, raised it to 53,000! Only the intervention of a later legislature, then a 1990 Initiative by the people, brought it down. Arkansas, too, had to face a federal judge who intervened for the people when that state went from "zero" signatures all the way up to 42,644 in 1970, only to have the courts knock down their little plot.

One of the ways to counterbalance arrogant party power is the Initiative, the chance for voters to put laws on the ballot themselves through a petition. But here, too, party bosses of both parties have put in giant roadblocks.

The Initiative, which became popular in the progressive era of Teddy Roosevelt and Bob La Follette, swept much of the Western states. But it did not make much headway in the East and Midwest, where politics was already the entrenched province of machine party politicians.

Today, there are only twenty-four states, mainly west of the Mississippi, where the people can overrule the politicians. These Initiative "propositions" supercede the narrow, often lobby-dictated vision of most legislators, which is why they fight so hard against the idea. Once passed, neither the governor nor the legislature can usually change it. The people's will is paramount.

(Unfortunately, the power-mad courts are interfering

against the people by overruling some Initiatives, especially the controversial ones. Although Prop 187 in California, which limits social services for illegal immigrants, won overwhelmingly at the ballot box, the courts are holding it up.)

In the last fifty years, only two states have granted the Initiative to citizens. Voters of our sample state, Connecticut, were promised the Initiative by the new governor, John Rowland, but nothing has happened. If they were granted it, polls indicate that Connecticut citizens would vote out the state income tax and replace it with a rise in sales tax. But they can't because politicians and their parties are jealous of granting any power to the voters.

A New Debate

The Initiative has become particularly important because of a debate that has put voters and politicians at loggerheads over a touchy issue—term limits. The nation has overwhelmingly shown that it wants to eliminate most of the "professionalism" in politics. By limiting how long a politician can serve in any one office, voters hope they will be forced to return to normal civilian life.

But politicians in both the Democratic and Republican Parties have locked arms on term limits, working together to defy the public.

Only through the Initiative have voters been able to express themselves on this issue. Propositions for term limits have been put on the ballot by citizens in twenty-three states, and despite heavy politician opposition, have passed with an average two-thirds vote.

The public knows that the longer a politician stays in office, the more likely he is to conform to the party establishment and to respect the status quo. A *Los Angeles Times-Mirror* poll showed that 78 percent of citizens believe politicians quickly lose touch with their constituents. It's also expensive. Congressmen who are in office five years or longer vote to spend more money than freshmen, who can still remember their civilian life, where a buck is still a buck, not a fanciful "appropriation."

But people in most states—such as New York and New Jersey—don't have the simple right of Initiative, and thus can't vote on term limits. In every state legislature (except recently in Mississippi) the Democrats and Republicans entered a quiet conspiracy to defeat the reform.

And where it has passed by voter Initiative, politicians, including former Speaker of the House Tom Foley, have challenged it. The Supreme Court has declared term limits passed by states to be unconstitutional for elected federal officials. But term limits for local and state officials have been upheld. In those states, politicians must seek a different office or return to civilian life—where they belong.

In Congress, term limits was on the Contract with America, but enough Republicans deserted their leaders to join the Democrats and defeat it. One wonders if it wasn't only a "loss leader" to gain support for the Contract, and was never intended to pass.

A Needed Amendment

The answer to term limits for House and Senate members is obvious: a constitutional amendment like the 22nd, which now restricts presidents from serving more than two terms. Such a law is needed to control members of Congress, especially as Americans become increasingly convinced that the present system of representative government is not working well. Since the mess is the politician's product, more power has to be transferred directly to the American voter if we are to straighten out governmental failure.

A new constitutional amendment should limit *all* politicians, from town and state officers to members of the U.S. Senate, to two terms, with only one exception: Members of the House should be allowed three terms of two years each. By rotating our politicians, we eliminate those for whom elections are life and death. We also nourish the skeptical citizen's point of view that spending money and passing more complex legislation is not the goal of civilization.

"If Congress doesn't pass a constitutional amendment to limit their terms," warns Norm Leahy of the U.S. Term Limits, "we may have to call a constitutional convention, which the Constitution sets up at the request of two-thirds of the states, and get it done there."

Professional politicians band together like thieves to make it difficult for independents to run against them, as we have seen. But neither are they generous with members of their own party unless they have worked their way up the ladder, a blatant "clubism" that has to be eliminated.

How? By simple arithmetic—by reducing the large number of signatures now needed to get on the party primary ballot for Congress, for example.

Easy Ballot

There is one state in the Union that has outflanked the party bosses.

That state is Ohio. Under Ohio statutes, *anyone* registered in the party can run for the U.S. Congress as a representative, and that includes any citizen who never stepped foot in a clubhouse. It's a simple matter of numbers, an equation that cuts through party mumbo-jumbo. In Ohio, *it takes only fifty signatures* to get on the party primary ballot for the House, a system that should be copied throughout the nation if we want to empower the voter.

(Anyone who can't get fifty signatures of friends, neighbors and fellow workers doesn't belong in politics.)

The major parties are excellent conspirators, especially against people who would like to oppose them as Independents or as members of a third party. Independents and the "Unaffiliated," as some states call those not registered in any party, are the stepchildren of democracy even though they are America's largest group—and growing.

According to the National Elections Center at the University of Michigan, 37 percent of Americans label themselves "Independents," while 36 percent are Democrats and 29 percent Republicans. This is a 50 percent jump for Independents since 1952, when only 23 percent called themselves "Independents." Using a simple graph, by the next generation, Independents will dominate the political landscape—a glimpse of which we saw in the Perot movement.

How do the parties hope to stop the trend? Not by getting close to the public, but by using their control of the state legislatures to keep the Independents from ever gaining power. Again, simple arithmetic is wheeled into place to shoot down the enemy. In the State of Florida, as we've seen, it takes 200,000 signatures to get on the state ballot, a near-impossibility for a new or small party. Other states have equally punishing limits.

To get around this, we need a new math, something akin to the Ohio law. That was the goal of Congressman John Conyers, Democrat of Michigan, who proposed House Resolution 1582, which would make third party and independent runs for federal office quite possible.

Under his bill, it would take a maximum of only 1,000 signatures, for example, to run for the U.S. Senate in any state, and as little as one-tenth of 1 percent in smaller states.

In states like New Hampshire, with some 500,000 actual voters, one could run for the Senate with only 500 signatures on the petition. This would leave to the people the decision of whether an individual should be taken as seriously as the major party candidates who are automatically placed on the ballot.

What has happened to Conyer's bill? Naturally, it was stomped to death in committee by both the Elephant and the Donkey.

The Unequal College

The political parties can't be blamed for the beginnings of another inequality in the system—the Electoral College, which was set up in the Constitution in Article II, Section IV. But they can be blamed for keeping it in place even though times have passed it by. And as we shall see, they have twisted it around to suit their own purposes.

The Electoral College, in which a majority of electors, not a majority of the voters, name the president, was instituted by the Founding Fathers as a compromise between central control of the federal government and the rights of states. The Constitution sets up the number of electors in each state as being equal to the combined number of senators and representatives from the state. That makes a total of 535, to which legislation has added three more from the District of Columbia.

Under our system, the president is not really elected on the first Tuesday after the first Monday in November. On Election Day we vote only for electors, who then meet in their respective statehouses on the second Wednesday in December. Then, on January 6 of the following year, the President Pro Tem of the U.S. Senate, in front of a joint session of Congress, counts the tally of the Electoral College and names the president.

Initially, the people did not even elect the electors who elected the president. That was done by the state legislatures. Then, a little at a time, voters were given that right, and have it today—in a way. (Members of the U.S. Senate only began to be elected by popular vote beginning with the Seventeenth Amendment in 1913.)

An interesting aspect is that the Constitution does not bind electors to the presidential candidate they are pledged to. However, almost all—with a few historic exceptions—do.

But majority rule of the citizens still doesn't rule today. Three times in history, as schoolchildren *used* to know, Andrew Jackson, Samuel Tilden and Grover Cleveland who won the popular vote in America, lost the electoral vote and did not become president that term.

Sometimes the system is even more twisted. Take the election of 1992. There were three major candidates: Bill Clinton, George Bush and Ross Perot. Clinton received 43 percent of the popular vote. Fifty-seven percent voted against him, but he became president because he won 68 percent of the electoral votes—the eleventh time in history this has happened.

How was that spread of twenty-five points between the popular and Electoral College vote possible? Simply because of another two-party conspiracy unrelated to constitutional provisions. The Constitution leaves it to the state legislatures to decide how the electoral votes for their state shall be counted. In effect, they have three choices:

1. Proportionately for each candidate in relation to their popular vote.
2. By electing electors from each congressional district, then two at large.
3. Winner take all for the entire state, no matter how small a percentage plurality the candidate receives.

Forty-eight of the states, unfortunately, have adopted No. 3, bringing in a grave distortion of democracy. Only

Maine and Nebraska have broken from the sheepish pack and split the electoral votes the way they were intended (but not stated), which is by congressional district, or even by No. 1, proportionately throughout the state.

Strange Spread

It's the present politician-party-controlled method of choosing electors that often creates the ridiculous spread between popular and electoral vote.

If, for instance, the states had adopted rule No. 1, then Clinton would probably not have achieved a majority of the Electoral College and the race would have been thrown into the House of Representatives by constitutional edict. The result? Mr. Perot would have been in the contest in the House, along with George Bush, and theoretically could have been named president. Clinton still would have been elected president by the Democratic House in 1992. But had the election been held in 1994, with a Republican-controlled House, George Bush would have been reelected.

If the statehouse politicians would choose No. 1 or No. 2 instead of their present "winner take all" method of naming electors, then we'd probably never have politicians take the Oval Office without a majority of the voters, as they regularly do today.

In such a case, according to the Constitution, the House determines the president from the *three* leading candidates. Regardless of population, each state has only one vote. Today, giant California and small Delaware would have the same single vote. The first candidate to receive twenty-six votes is named president of the United States.

The first case of a presidential election in which no one gained a majority of the electors was in 1800, when Jefferson and Aaron Burr tied in the Electoral College for the presidency. After several votes in the House, Jefferson was chosen president by a vote of 10 to 4. Aaron Burr was named vice president.

The eccentric rule at the time was that the man with the second highest vote became vice president. This was repealed by the Twelfth Amendment, passed in 1804, which set up the present system, as flawed as it is.

The second time no one achieved an electoral majority for president was in 1824, in a four-way race between Andrew Jackson, John Quincy Adams, William Crawford and Henry Clay. Jackson, Old Hickory and victor of the battle of New Orleans, won the popular vote but did not gain a majority of the electors and the race was thrown into the House.

Clay, who came in fourth and was thus not eligible, threw his votes to Adams, who was elected president even though he had lost the popular election. In return, Adams named Clay secretary of state, a deal which was dubbed "The Corrupt Bargain."

John C. Calhoun of South Carolina, a vice presidential candidate running under no party, did win a majority of the electors and did not have to submit to a congressional vote. For VP in such cases, the Constitution sets up a contest in the Senate, not the House, among the top two, not the top three, vote-getters.

An Anachronism

That system may have fit that time in history, but today it's a nonsensical, antidemocratic anachronism, and not worthy of a great nation. It turns all third-party candidates into "spoilers." It robs the people of true choice and often elects a president who has been rejected by a majority of the voters.

The solution?

Easy. I propose a 29th Amendment to the Constitution, which I will describe in detail (see Chapter 8), designed to correct *all* the undemocratic practices in both parties.

These aberrations have been created by the selfish, narrow vision of the two major parties of America: the Donkey and the Elephant. To reduce their influence and increase that of the American voter will require drastic changes in our laws. Without those reforms, the Republic will continue to flounder.

With them, we can restore, ensure and advance our natural greatness.

5

THE MIDDLE-CLASS MANIFESTO

What the People Want—and Politicians Don't Understand

We've seen how most American politicians become expert at raising money, sometimes unethically, and getting themselves elected and reelected to office. We've also seen how some in their ranks bend and break the law to enrich themselves. Now we need to look at whether our politicians have shown enough insight and intelligence to ensure America's health, societally and economically.

The answer is a decided "no."

The elected and appointed officials of our two political parties in which we have invested so much energy, time and money have failed us again. They have taken America's natural formula for success—an abundant spirit, social mobility, a tradition of extraordinary creativity and a love of freedom ingrained in our Constitution—and turned it upside down.

Over the last thirty years, our politicians (federal, state and local) have given us a series of irrational laws and taxes that have accomplished what no foreign enemy could. They have transformed our horn of plenty and Jefferson's pursuit of happiness into a distorted vision.

Insisting that their way, and not the people's, be enforced, they are turning America into a nation riven by social and economic unrest.

Is it a conspiracy of evil? Of course not.

However, it is a conspiracy of willful ignorance, one against the common sense of the people, who, not surprisingly, seem to know better than the Political Class.

Gullible Public

Our politicians have used their skill at rhetoric and as entertainers (actually, second-class actors; the superior ones go to Hollywood) to convince the gullible American public that slow growth, unemployment, punishing taxes, class conflict and discord are all natural by-products of complicated modern society.

Nothing could be farther from the truth. America should be twice as prosperous and stable as it is today—if the people had their way.

Do the people really know what they want? a cynic might ask.

"Yes."

What they want is not codified in law, and it's only partially represented by the two major parties. It's not liberal, conservative or even middle of the road. It is a quiet, almost secret consensus, but it is not difficult to uncover if one knows where to look.

It is a Middle-Class Manifesto, a populist platform whose wisdom resides in the working bourgeoisie, the much-maligned middle class which produces virtually all the money and talent that drives the nation. Unfortunately, they and their ideas are poorly represented by the ruling elites.

One reason PROFESSIONAL POLITICIANS have made such a mess is that they operate under the theory that only the manic passage of legislation and programs can benefit the people, as if the sheer *volume* of laws was essential to our survival.

In 1995, for example, the House passed some seven hundred bills. What if, over the last thirty years, they had been less frenetic? Would America be worse or better off today? I would say better, especially if we keep in mind the vital dictum: *Primum Non Nocere*—First Do No Harm.

Take the federal budget of 1950. If we extrapolate it, with inflation, to 1996, we would now be spending only $800 billion a year, *half* as much as today's bloated Washington expenditures. And remember: For every piece of congressional legislation, there's an equal executive branch response in setting up bureaucracies and regulations.

Is it possible that the enormous time and energy spent on new legislation is itself destructive?

New Hampshire thinks so. Their large citizen legislature works only a brief maximum forty-five day fling in Concord. They're paid $100 and then they return home.

These populist lawmakers have kept the state the best tax haven in the nation, with neither a state income tax nor a sales tax.

The American people intuitively know that low taxation means more business, an idea which escapes most politicians. Texas and Florida, which have no state income tax, are creating jobs twice as fast as the rest of the nation. And people elsewhere vote with their feet, leaving high tax areas such as Connecticut and New York (the two worst) to go elsewhere. Connecticut is one of only two states to have actually lost population since 1990, the other being Rhode Island, with New York close behind. High-taxed Californians are massively migrating to Nevada, Utah and Idaho.

In the obverse of New Hampshire's lawmakers, the handsomely paid U.S. Congress ($133,000 a year) has a record that I need not reiterate. Its abysmal performance over the last thirty years, combined with the inadequacy of the Oval Office—no matter which party occupied it—has slowly sapped our self-confidence and historic magnificence.

People's Equation

What if the people were *directly* in charge of the political system? What would they do instead? Is there a magical equation for success that cuts across party lines?

I believe there is.

Why should the people have this superior knowledge? Simply because they are on the firing line, where the party rhetoric counts for little. The people's views are not only more pragmatic but, in a strange sense, more intelligent.

(Unfortunately, they don't always vote their knowledge. Americans are often naive and easily swayed by political lies and humbug. Being honest themselves, they cannot imagine that anyone else could lie as facilely as do some politicians.)

So what is this secret consensus of the people, which, if enacted, would make America bloom like cherry blossoms in March? It can only be described as a MIDDLE-CLASS MANIFESTO.

It's related to an age-old tradition of "populism." What is populism? The phrase means of the people, and as the dictionary explains its political connotation: "policies that appeal to the common man rather than the traditional party or partisan ideologies."

Populism is a term that's seldom heard when representative government is working well. Populist ideas become a rallying cry only when dissatisfaction is high and politicians are not doing their job. We are living in just such a time.

Populism has been the claim of both the left wing and the right wing over the years, but the true populist movement is ideologically neither left, right nor center. It is designed to block the entrenched special interests, whether economic or political, operating against the majority of the people.

Early Populism

The first large-scale movement was spearheaded by the People's Party, also known as the Populist Party. A revolt in the 1890s by farmers against the eastern money interests, it also attracted city people who wanted equal opportunity.

In 1892, they won twenty-two electoral votes in the presidential election, some congressional seats and many statewide offices. In fact, the Populists took over the Democratic Party convention in 1896 and, adding their cause to the party platform, nominated William Jennings Bryan.

Since then, it has had several messengers, each tackling a portion of the true agenda: Bob La Follette, Teddy Roosevelt, FDR, all the way up to Ross Perot. LBJ considered himself a populist, but it was his deficit spending in a period of affluence that started the avalanche of debt and big government that now threatens the middle class.

Today, populism is not the voice of farmers but of the middle-class workers and the self-employed, whether white collar or blue, who are just beginning to understand their mutual dependence, whether they make $20,000 or $100,000. They are all victims of the current job loss epidemic and structural economic decay. Overtaxed and insecure, they are truly pessimistic about the future for the first time.

Collectively, they are subject to the will of the political and economic "elites"—the politicians, the bureaucrats at every level, the banks, the multinational corporations, the lobbyists, the media, even the legal and medical professions. These selfish groups consider themselves sophisticated, and are generally well educated in a modern sense, but they have few answers to the nation's problems. The solutions they do advance make little sense to the family in the trenches.

If ever a nation needed a populist middle-class movement, it is at this juncture in our history. That doesn't necessarily mean that there must be a POPULIST PARTY, at least until the political structure is remodeled to make a third party a viable constitutional force instead of a "spoiler" (see Chapter 8).

But it does mean that most of our present economic and social policies must be reexamined and that solutions should be advanced.

I've outlined many of these problems and solutions in my three books on government: *The Government Racket: Washington Waste A to Z; A Call for Revolution: How Washington Is Strangling America;* and *The Tax Racket: Government Extortion From A to Z.* Now, I'll try to integrate those ideas, add new facts and new issues and bring the people's argument up to the present.

The MIDDLE-CLASS MANIFESTO could be endless, but I have summarized eleven major points. Here, then, is a list of what modern populism could do to rescue America from itself.

I. Political Reform

The desire for reform unites almost all populist groups, which believe in making the system more democratic and chasing the money changers from the Political Temple. I've already expressed some recommendations in this book, and many more will follow.

II. A Balanced Budget; Pay Down of Debt

In 1996, almost 60 percent of personal income taxes will go just to pay the interest on the national debt. We can't continue in this vein. The first step is, of course, a balanced budget, something several politicians have blocked through their exaggerated rhetoric about the danger of reducing social programs. This is pure demagoguery and should not be taken seriously.

Once the balanced budget is achieved, we must begin to pay down the national debt, which will reach $6 trillion by 2002—if we don't have a recession first.

Traditionally, we created a budget surplus in good years, such as the 1920s, then a deficit in such down years as the Great Depression. Only since JFK, and following through with all Democratic and Republican administrations (with the exception of 1969), have we borrowed in periods of affluence. This is the work of morally weak and perhaps ignorant politicians, of whom we have an abundant number.

III. Term Limits

The crying need for term limits is obvious. We must dispatch PROFESSIONAL POLITICIANS and replace them with ordinary citizens serving temporarily—with no retirement pensions other than Social Security. They should graciously return home at the end of their term and not be allowed to stay in Washington as lobbyists (see Chapter 7).

Unfortunately, the Supreme Court has ruled that state legislatures and Initiative votes by the people can only limit the term of officeholders within a state, from the office of governor down. They cannot control congressional terms. Our answer should be enormous public pressure to force Congress to pass legislation or a constitutional amendment to limit their own terms. If that doesn't succeed, two thirds of the states might have to call a constitutional convention and do it themselves.

IV. Lower Taxes, Fairer System

The present system unfairly penalizes the middle class. The IRS code sets rates so high that the typical family pays at a level once reserved for the rich. One result is that most families need two paychecks to survive.

The fifteen-thousand-page tax code is unfair. At $40,000 in taxable income, hardly a fortune, federal income rates jump to 28 percent, but politicians love to forget the nondeductible FICA tax, which is really a disguised second income tax. When we add it in, that places earnings of up to $62,700, the Social Security maximum in 1996, into the high 35.65 federal marginal rate. And as you go up in income, the rates rise quickly to 31, even 36 percent. With FICA taxes, and no ceiling on Medicare taxes, that puts upper-middle-class people in the 40 to 45 percent federal bracket.

It's considerably worse for the self-employed, who pay 41.3 percent in federal taxes once they reach the exalted taxable income of $40,000!

On top of that, most Americans pay some thirty other taxes, including state income taxes, often local income or payroll taxes, state sales tax, local sales tax, school tax, town and county property taxes, bridge and highway tolls, gas taxes, excise taxes, airplane taxes, personal property (car) taxes, FCC telephone tax, ad infinitum.

The typical family now pays more in taxes than for food, housing and medical care combined. Those who do relatively well are pushed into the *red zone*, the almost 50 percent marginal range.

This is more than punishment from the government; it is an evil policy. But politicians who are destroying the family's economic well-being through excessive taxes apparently feel no shame. (Perhaps that's the defining difference between politicians and us ordinary people.)

The politician's contemporary solution—an extra $500 tax credit per child—is not only meaningless, it's also insulting.

The ultimate goal must be a 25 percent tax cut, federal, state and local—across the board. That depends on large reductions in the budgets of our 85,000 wasteful governments, a process that will take a generation and an awakened public. Until that time, we can at least change the system to make it less unfair.

Two Alternatives

Two major changes have been suggested: the Flat Tax and the National Sales Tax.

The Flat Tax, which played a part in the Republican presidential primaries because of Steve Forbes, has gotten the most publicity. In the House, it is being pushed by Dick Armey, the Republican majority leader.

It sounds attractive, and it *might* work, but it has several grave problems which must be fixed if it is ever to become law.

1. The postcard filing is a sham unless legislation blocks the IRS from auditing *everyone*. For workers with only wages, filing is no problem under the present system or under the Flat Tax. But what about the hardware store owner who grosses $600,000 but puts down the only item asked for—his net earning of $60,000? Will the IRS believe him, or any of the millions of self-employed and others with additional income who will also deliver a one-line declaration?

Probably not. The IRS audited over a million Americans in 1994, and more than 2 million in 1995, when Congress gave them additional funds. Under the Flat Tax, will the number of audits jump to 10 million so that the suspicious IRS can intrude even further into our lives? If we ever do have a Flat Tax, we must first curb the IRS inquisitors.

So instead of "killing" the IRS, as some Flat Tax proponents falsely claim, it could make it more onerous than ever. And no Flat Tax eliminates the $23 billion in penalties and billions more in interest that Americans pay the IRS each year.

2. The second problem is the home mortgage tax deduction, which many proponents of the Flat Tax want to eliminate. Over 60 percent of Americans own their own home, a movement stimulated by the tax break on mortgage interest deductions. Take that away and no one knows what will happen to home prices and home ownership.

Also, there is a geographical distortion in losing that deduction. A typical home mortgage in Arkansas may be

$50,000, while it is more likely $200,000 in California or in the metropolitan New York or Boston areas. So?

So the tax money will flow to poorer, lower-home-cost areas away from the large metropolitan areas where houses are relatively expensive.

3. Most proposals of a Flat Tax also eliminate the present deduction for property and school taxes. That, too, is unfair geographically. A home in Little Rock averages under $1,000 a year property tax, while it's closer to $5,000 on Long Island. With this deduction eliminated, the money again flows from high tax areas to less expensive ones throughout the nation.

4. Right now, we can deduct our state income taxes as well, which in states like California, New York, Connecticut and New Jersey, as well as many others, are onerous. However, Florida and Texas have no state income taxes and therefore residents there will gain under the Flat Tax at the expense of residents of the forty-three states that do. So in both 2, 3 and 4, the geographic socioeconomic differences make the Flat Tax unfair.

5. The truly rich will make out like proverbial bandits. Not only will their rates go down enormously, but they will pay no taxes on interest and "coupon" income, which adds a further burden to the burdened middle class.

IF we can correct 1, 2, 3, 4 and 5, a modified Flat Tax with those deductions is better than the present convoluted tax system and the IRS code. But if not, it will skew it in ways we still can't appreciate.

A Possible Solution

So, is there a solution to the present tax problem?

Yes, there is. It is quite simple. It is a constitutional amendment, now contemplated by Bill Archer of Texas, chairman of the House Ways and Means Committee, to PERMANENTLY close the IRS.

What will replace it? A simple National Sales Tax.

No one will file anything with Washington, and people's income will be their own business. There will be no direct federal income taxes. Is it possible to collect enough money to initiate such a Nirvana?

Absolutely. The Form 1040 that most of us fill out collected $543 billion in 1994 from wages, royalties, self-employed income, capital gains, inheritance tax and the earnings of small-business people, including those incorporated as Sub Chapter S firms.

To bring in the same amount of money, all we need is a 13.5 percent tax on all goods and services, with the exception of food, housing and medical care in order to protect the poor.

But, say critics, a National Sales Tax is regressive, that is, it hurts the poor. But it need not be. Right now, FICA (Social Security and Medicare) is the most regressive tax there is. A teenager who works at McDonald's now pays $800 a year he can't afford in FICA taxes. Under the sales tax plan, there's an easy replacement in which he'll pay nothing. By adding 6 percent to the 13.5, or a total of 19.5 percent, we can eliminate the employee's end of FICA, and still bring in all the money that Social Security and Medicare require.

Without the FICA deduction, Washington won't be taking a penny out of our paychecks. The ability to control our own taxes by what we spend will free us up, financially and psychologically. No more bookkeeping for the government, no more filing, no more audits, no more penalties and interest, no more liens and seizures, no more saving of receipts and no more paying H & R Block, or a more expensive tax consultant. No more fear of Washington. No more intrusion into our lives.

Rosy Future

I anticipate that such a plan will trigger the greatest affluence in our history, rivaling the 1950s, already a legendary period when Washington was more theater than penalizer.

The National Sales Tax has other values. At present, the IRS estimates that $127 billion is lost through evasion each year. Arthur Little, the survey firm in Cambridge, Massachusetts, has estimated that the mere act of record keeping and filing with the IRS is costing the nation $200 billion a year. Those two items eat up more than 50 percent of all monies collected.

Under a National Sales Tax plan, there will be no filing costs, and evasion will be cut in half or better. Even criminals will be taxed when they buy their Lexuses and Rolexes. Our present experience shows that there is less evasion in state sales taxes than in income taxes, and we can anticipate the same when we institute it on a national level.

But who would collect the funds?

Right now, forty-five states have a sales tax. The

same people would collect the National Sales Tax—and receive a fee for their efforts.

There's another unexpected blessing of a National Sales Tax. Washington will have to suffer as we do during a recession. If we have less, we'll buy less, forcing the federal government to enter the real world for the first time. Staff, programs, salaries will have to be cut back. They will no longer be immune to the hardships they create.

But won't they just raise the sales tax rate if they need money, say during a recession?

No, that's the wonderful subtlety of the plan. It's market driven, not politician driven. If rates get too high, people will buy less and Washington will get still less revenue than before. And if rates are too high, Mr. Ford and Mr. General Motors will scream bloody murder, and their complaints register more quickly than yours or mine.

If Americans want to control their politicians, instead of being controlled by them—as we are now—then the National Sales Tax is the only ticket.

For the next decade, pundits and politicians will argue. But I can assure you that as long as we have an IRS and politicians working in concert, the era of true American affluence and growth will be over. Remember: All great civilizations have been destroyed by excessive and unfair taxation.

V. Cut Overblown Government and Waste

Populists are in full agreement: The American government at all levels is too large and too inefficient. It takes too much out of the economy and delivers too little to the working middle class.

This is a massive subject that I have explored several times, but I can give you a snapshot of the problem and some of the things that need to be done.

Manpower

The only reasonable change since 1993 has been the reduction of the federal employee pool by 200,000. (Most other serious cuts passed by Congress have been vetoed by the President.) We haven't even noticed that the employees are gone. There are some 1.9 million federal civilian workers left. How many do we really need?

Probably half of them. Remember, most are not hard-working, essential manpower. To be conservative, we can easily part with one third. Each employee costs us $85,000 a year in *cash* for salary, benefits and pensions, not counting some trillion dollars in unfunded pensions collectively.

(Government employees make 45 percent more than those in private industry, and receive 75 percent more in pensions and benefits.)

Eliminating 600,000 people through attrition, without laying anyone off, is easy. Seven percent of government employees leave, die or retire each year. Even if we rehire some "essential" workers, we will reduce the staff by 5 percent per year.

In approximately seven years, the year of the supposed balanced budget, we'll have cut almost all the 600,000, saving $50 billion a year immediately, and much more later in continuing benefits and pensions.

Can we lose those people? Happily. The Department of Agriculture, for example, has some sixty thousand people who oversee the fake conservation work and the subsidy system. The subsidies are scheduled to be eliminated over a seven-year period, and so should the people. They even have two thousand home economists who no longer visit the farms. What they do no one seems to know.

In the Defense Department during World War II, we had one civilian for each five servicemen. In 1970, we had 1.2 million civilian employees in defense and 3 million servicemen, a ratio of almost one to three. Although the military personnel have now been cut down to 1.8 million, we still have 900,000 civilian employees, one for each two servicemen. If we continue at this rate, there will soon be one civilian DOD employee for each serviceman—perhaps able to carry his carbine into combat.

We can safely cut 300,000 civilian employees just in the DOD, again through attrition. (Perhaps we could *increase* the number of servicemen by 100,000 at the same time.) By cutting out another 300,000 civilians in the other agencies, we'll have achieved our goal of 600,000 fewer people living off the taxpayers.

In all, there are 19 million government employees in America. By eliminating 25 percent of them from the statehouse to the county seat, solely through attrition, we'll save an additional $300 billion a year! And I can assure you of one thing: They'll never be missed.

Overhead

"We've never done a study of the overhead of the United States government," says a spokesman for the Office of Management and Budget (OMB), who suffers no shame making that extraordinary statement.

But Congressman Lamar Smith of Texas has studied it. "The OMB threatened to physically throw us out of their library when we tried to learn the real overhead of the federal government," says John Lampmann, the congressman's aide. "But we found out, and it's outrageous."

A conservative estimate of the overhead is $240 billion a year, or $125,000 per employee, about three times that of private industry. Of this amount, more than half is called "Other Services" (No. 25.2 in the federal budget), an unexplained miscellaneous category for which the OMB will issue no figures. Basically, it's a "slush fund" that lets the cabinet agencies waste as much as they want, which is considerable.

With a one-third cut in manpower, we should be able to make at least a one-quarter cut in overhead, for a savings of $60 billion more a year.

Pork

This is a peculiarly American invention. The Constitution gives Congress the responsibility of appropriating money *to run the government*.

But in its infinite lack of wisdom, Congress spends multibillion dollars a year that have absolutely nothing to do with the government. Nowhere in the Constitution does it authorize them to spend money *extragovernmentally*—on gifts to friends, nonprofit groups, private businesses or local projects singled out without any law or pattern.

Yet almost every congressman worth a campaign contribution spends millions on pork. He uses his authority, generally as a member of one of the twenty-six appropriations committees in the House and Senate, to send checks (our money) back to his hometown in order to secure the love of his constituents and get himself reelected.

(It's called "pork," because at one time a barrel of salted pork was laid out at Christmastime for workers. Now the goodies are spread throughout the year.)

It's big business, it's blatantly corrupt, it robs the treasury, but it goes on regularly with no letup. What seems to be a free gift from the Treasury eventually makes everyone poorer, including those who receive it. Too easily, constituents forget that the same ridiculous gifts they receive are also being sent all over the nation.

Who can play? Virtually everyone. Eighty-four congressmen in the Senate and the House are members of appropriations committees, which puts many fingers in the national pie. And if a congressman is not a member of appropriations, he surely has friends who are.

In two of my previous books, I helped publicize this ridiculous behavior, which should be considered unethical but is actually praised by some as "constituent" concern.

Much of the money allocated is for projects so ludicrous that they make perfect fodder for critics of Congress, and rightly so. Here are some of the most recent "pork" goodies to add to those I've already explored over the years:

- $500,000 for the construction of the home of Charles Corneau, Abraham Lincoln's neighbor
- $4 million to teach "leadership" to college students
- $936,000 to the Palmer Chiropractic School to conduct demonstrations in Iowa
- $15 million for a footbridge from New Jersey to Ellis Island
- $1 million to restore the Allen Theater in Cleveland, Ohio
- $2 million for the Toledo (Ohio) Farmer's Market
- $1.2 million to St. Frances and St. Vincent Colleges in Pennsylvania for "global competitiveness studies"
- $1,395,000 for Indiana State University, the alma mater of a House appropriations committee member
- $6 million for the World University games in New York
- $19 million for the International Fund for Ireland, a program that has used taxpayer money for such things as a golf video center
- $1.6 million for a "congestion mitigation project" in Syracuse, New York
- $3 million for an Orlando, Florida, streetcar project
- $120 million for a courthouse in Phoenix, Arizona
- $96,390,000 for a courthouse in Portland, Oregon

- $4.2 million for a "National Conversation on Pluralism and Identity"
- $125,000 for a schoolteacher summer program to "study the role of photography in forming an American identity"
- $161,913 to study "Israeli Reactions to SCUD Attacks" (They didn't like them.)
- $104,055 to study how people communicate through facial expressions
- $77,826 for "Coping with Change in Czechoslovakia"
- $124,910 to find ways to reduce "school phobia" among youngsters (Don't give them any homework.)
- $105,163 to study the "Evolution of Monogamy in Biparental Rodents"
- $5.1 million to build a *third* golf course at Andrews Air Force Base near Washington, the site of the plush federal airline for VIPs. It costs 6.5 million of our tax dollars every year to maintain the golf courses.

(The list of pork could fill page after page, and more can be studied by joining two public-spirited organizations: Citizens Against Government Waste in Washington, phone: 1-800-BE-ANGRY; and National Taxpayers Union, phone: 1-703-683-5700. Both are dedicated to protecting the abused taxpayer.)

No Controls

The tragedy is that there is no control on free-spending, unethical pork-happy congressmen. They can give money to *anyone* for any reason, which should not be permitted.

There is, surprisingly, an easy solution to the pork problem.

All we need is a House and Senate rule that prohibits any member of an appropriations committee from granting additional funds to his home district. And equally important, a second rule that will stop committee members from swapping pork with a colleague.

Any action in violation of this rule should be considered "unethical" behavior and subject the member to censure, or worse. Such discipline will save us between $10 and $20 billion a year and perhaps rehabilitate the reputation of Congress, if that's possible. As I've said before, professional politicians (and most turn "pro" quickly) are quite different from you and me.

These few insights illustrate the adolescent behavior of federal officials which has resulted in our bloated federal government. (Most state operations are not far behind.) To these, we can add unneeded cabinet agencies (Truman had eight; we now have fourteen!), overlap and duplication (job training is done in fourteen agencies; Indians are cared for by twelve), programs that are expanded when they fail, ad infinitum.

Government waste is ever-present and I expect our politicians will continue to provide us with fodder.

VI. Welfare

Nothing alienates working people more than the government's welfare program. Charity is inherent in our democracy and our Judeo-Christian culture. But welfare is not charity. It is the unconscionable taking of the hard-earned money of those who work and, in most cases, giving it to those who have found a way to give birth to children out of wedlock at the taxpayer's expense. Simultaneously, it removes them from the mainstream of American life.

Equally important to the burden it places on working people is that this cruel (not charitable) program destroys the very people it was intended to help. It is, plainly speaking, the government subsidization of promiscuity and illegitimacy. The resulting destruction of the nuclear family is the handiwork of politicians and bureaucrats who pretend to be compassionate but who are actually the sworn enemies of both those who pay and those who receive.

Who can achieve a middle-class existence on a welfare check?

No one. Its destructive power is shown in the statistics. Afro-American families, which had only 19 percent incidence of out-of-wedlock births after World War II, now suffer from a devastating rate of illegitimacy: 66 percent, most of it courtesy of "generous" Uncle Sam.

The numbers are almost as punishingly high for Hispanic-Americans, and the white community of European origin is catching up. In 1950, the out-of-wedlock birth rate was 2 percent; it is now approaching 20 percent, and continues to increase.

Enormous Cost

The cost of welfare is enormous and reported inaccurately by the media. To house, feed, clothe, heal and educate the poor in America costs $400 billion a year in eighty programs in six different uncoordinated cabinet departments and dozens of subagencies. According to the bipartisan Congressional Research Service, it is the nation's largest budget item.

There's an easy solution, one called "work." Despite false publicity, all current attempts to move people massively from welfare to work have failed. The reason is obvious. No one can compete with a free check. FDR realized that when he closed Home Relief, except for the truly disabled and widows, and substituted the WPA (Works Progress Administration) with jobs for everyone. Five million men joined, which would be equivalent to 12 million today.

To replicate that for the 5 million welfare families, mainly headed by women, would be relatively inexpensive, and actually save money in both the short and long run. *Without* additional education or training, welfare recipients can do needed work in hospitals, at day-care centers, as school aides, etcetera.

If each head of household received $15,000 a year plus health insurance, the total tab would be $100 billion, *much* less than we now spend on welfare families. A husband and wife on WPA could earn $30,000 together, plus health insurance. They would rise out of poverty, gain work habits and build families instead of fatherless homes.

As I've mentioned, the report that we spend $23

billion on Aid to Families with Dependent Children (AFDC) just includes the cash payments to welfare families. That cost *does not* cover food stamps, housing credits, Medicaid, WIC (Women, Infants, Children), plus scores of other programs, and the expensive administration of welfare bureaucrats and case workers at federal, state and local levels. Even if we provide day-care centers for working mothers with small children, the savings are large. Besides, the centers provide work for welfare mothers. Without checks for additional children, the number of out-of-wedlock births also declines, as New Jersey's new policy has shown.

Mathematics, I assure you, is not the strong suit of politicians.

The other dividend, which saves billions more, is that working families, as many studies show, produce children who commit less crime and have less drug dependency and less illegitimacy than those in welfare families. That social decay carries over to another generation—and another, and another.

There is no other answer except the WPA.

Not only the middle class should complain about the present waste of welfare money. The welfare recipients themselves should protest against being left out of real economy because of government shortsightedness in subsidizing the creation of fatherless families.

VII. Change Our Failed Trade Policy

American politicians have set up a false argument between FREE TRADE and PROTECTIONISM, which has confused the public, lost millions of jobs and threatens the future of trade.

What is the reality of so-called free trade? Closer examination shows that the true argument is between FAIR TRADE and RESTRICTED MARKETS, and between COMMON MARKETS WITH UNDEVELOPED COUNTRIES and COMMON MARKETS WITH DEVELOPED COUNTRIES.

Free trade between similar nations, with relatively similar wage scales, benefits both. Trade between America and Europe, for example, has traditionally been of value to both sides, with small surpluses and deficits which eventually cancel each other out.

We buy British woolens, German machines, French perfumes and wines and Italian fashions. Europeans buy our jet planes, Coca-Cola and movies.

But we have problems in other areas of the world, which we *must* correct. If we don't, we'll lose both our manufacturing base and the loyalty of American workers whose jobs are being shipped overseas.

Take Japan. In terms of wage costs, they are an ideal trading partner. It actually costs *more* to manufacture there than here, so we won't lose jobs based on just that factor. *But* Japan purposely RESTRICTS trade through government-approved feudal monopolistic schemes. Using them, they have built a $60 billion annual trade surplus with America, one which is draining our economy and destroying a number of our industries.

The answer to this trade challenge is not just to put in a tariff, which smacks of protectionism. Instead, in the case of Japan, we should RESTRICT the entry of their goods at exactly the same level they do ours. That is the ultimate measure of FAIR TRADE.

Low-wage countries are an equally severe problem. The answer there is to understand simple economics. You can buy and sell to them, but advanced countries cannot have a COMMON MARKET with a low-wage country. Period.

Manufacturing used to be difficult to transport. Today, with robotics and computers, and high-tech communications, it takes less than a year to duplicate quality manufacturing anywhere in the world.

Naturally, American and multinational firms are going to seek out cheap labor anywhere in the world to reduce the cost of their product, which is the obligation of a good capitalist—if we let him get away with it.

IF politicians are ignorant enough to set up a Common Market with a low-wage nation—Mexico, for example, as NAFTA hopes to do—simple arithmetic will give you an accurate portrait of the future. If the average manufacturing wage in America is $10 an hour, and it's $1 an hour in Mexico, then twenty-five years from now, you can project the manufacturing wage in America by this equation:

ADD TEN AND ONE, WHICH GIVES YOU ELEVEN. DIVIDE BY TWO AND YOU GET $5.50 AN HOUR.

Add one dollar for the convenience of staying here, and you come up with $6.50 an hour for American workers. Hardly the American Dream.

The China Problem

China is now rivaling Japan in terms of unfair trade. In their case it stems from an enormous wage differential which attracts American firms. We also face certain restrictions put on our trade by the Chinese government. The argument American politicians use to avoid facing the enormous trade deficit with China (now $35 billion and growing) is to say: You can buy your clothes, toys, clothes, etcetera, cheaper because of China.

Certainly, but if you don't have a job, you can't eat, let alone buy toys. We have the same problem with other Asian low-wage nations, which are now also gobbling up American jobs.

The conclusion: America can *only* have a Common Market (which is the better definition of treaties like NAFTA) with nations of a similar economy and personal incomes. We have to make sure that all low-wage countries bring in their goods, including goods made for American firms, with a *wage-differential tax*, which will discourage the export of our jobs. If this violates the trade agreements, they, not the American economy, must be changed.

BUT the untutored (most American politicians), and those determined to exploit American workers with low wages or by shipping their jobs overseas in exchange for cheap foreign labor, are destroying our chance for FAIR TRADE without a giant deficit.

They claim that we'll retrain American workers who have been left out of the American dream and bring them along on the information superhighway. That's fine for the educated, but for the many millions who will always want and need blue-collar work, we have the worst training and secondary school system in the Western world. If we have to rely on educators to salvage our jobs and America, we can kiss it all good-bye.

So, if you want to stop the demagoguery on both sides of the trade issue, let's brush up on basic Economics 101, and save the manufacturing base of America. I think we'll wake up one day and realize that we desperately need it.

VIII. Revamp a Failing Social Security

The Social Security program is in constant crisis, which causes grave concern among the middle class, who rely on it heavily for their retirement.

Unfortunately, it has been horribly mismanaged by politicians, who treat it as a fiscal toy rather than a sacred vehicle for the security of the aged—not only today but in future generations as well.

The problem started in 1935 when FDR set up Social Security and failed to segregate the FICA money from the general treasury, which meant that it was never truly invested. The present crisis began in 1983, when, fearing the insolvency of the program, Washington raised FICA taxes 25 percent to generate a giant surplus, supposedly to be used for the baby boomers when they came on line beginning in 2010.

They did produce the surplus, which was $70 billion in 1996. In all, by 2010, the tax hike and delayed benefits (retirement at sixty-seven), will generate a surplus of over *$2 trillion.* We were led to believe that the money would be sitting there, ready to pay out to the retired baby boomers.

Has it worked out that way? Hardly.

There won't be a nickel in the till—just IOUs that we all have to redeem with still another payment. What the government did, and does, is take the entire surplus and put it in the government's swampy general fund, where it is spent on such things as farm subsidies, limousines, welfare and benefits for unneeded bureaucrats. The money that is "borrowed" from FICA is then added to the national debt, to be paid back by the taxpayers.

BUT the deceitful government does not count the "borrowed" surplus in the deficit, a budget gimmick to make the deficit look smaller than it truly is.

Failure to Balance

As I have already mentioned, when the magic year 2002 comes, the budget will *not* be balanced. It will be $112 billion in the red—the surplus of Social Security that year taken and used up in the general fund, or as I am wont to say, "stolen."

When Tom Foley was Speaker, the Republicans accused the Democrats of playing hanky-panky with the Social Security surplus. Now that the Republicans are in power, the Democrats accuse Speaker Gingrich of doing the same.

And guess what? They're both right.

What does Social Security get in return? A nonnegotiable IOU from Uncle Sam. Who pays it back? The same taxpayers who paid excessive taxes to create the surplus in the first place. Soon we'll have to come up with $2 trillion so that the checks to boomers won't bounce when it comes retirement time. So the FICA taxpayer, and that's everyone, has to pay twice—if we're lucky.

(In the nongovernmental world, this would be considered a first cousin to the Ponzi scheme and rewarded with a little time at Leavenworth.)

What will happen beginning in 2010 if we don't change the system—now? We'll have to increase the FICA taxes, push the retirement age to seventy or go out and borrow more money, creating an enormous new deficit.

How do they get away with it? They lie, then have the nerve to shout down those few congressmen, including Senator Pat Moynihan, who suggest cutting the FICA taxes back until such time as we need the money. After all, critics say, we're taking the money out of the Social Security and Medicare "funds" and spending it on things other than the aged and disabled anyway.

What should be done to really save Social Security? I outlined that three years ago, and I shall repeat and add to the obvious solution. It's one which politicians have ignored for as long as they could.

The money should be truly *invested*, and not in rhetoric or government IOUs. For example, had some of the Social Security money been invested a generation ago in Ginnie Mae, Sally Mae, Freddy Mac and other securities that are implicitly guaranteed by the federal government, there would be no crisis, no raise in FICA taxes and the average check of $700 a month would probably be at least 50 percent larger.

Plan for Today

How about today? Is it too late to bring reason to the Social Security system?

Not if we follow a simple program.

1. Pass a law making it illegal for the government to put any of the surplus Social Security funds (over a half trillion dollars to date) into the general fund. The surplus must be sequestered, or the taxes reduced to the amount of the surplus, which runs about 15 percent per year.

2. Take the surplus and immediately invest it in government-guaranteed agencies like Ginnie Mae, or in top-rated municipal bonds.

3. Face up to the true deficit by adding the money borrowed from Social Security to it. Instead of a $160 billion a year deficit in 1995, we had a $225 billion deficit. A good reality check.

4. Change the balanced budget deal to eliminate that borrowed surplus within seven years so that Social Security will no longer be used as an escape valve for the overspent general fund. That means cuts in government of an additional $650 billion over seven years instead of just the $900 billion the Congress has planned.

5. Start the individualization of Social Security accounts, giving each person a separate number and a separate annual reckoning of the value of his account. Leave enough in the collective fund to handle the other insurance values, such as disability, widows' pensions, etcetera. Figure a thirty-year transition from the present system to one in which everyone will have his own full retirement account, much like a 401-K.

6. Beginning immediately, have every FICA payer

be able to take 10 percent of his and his employer's share and invest it privately in mutual funds, government-protected corporations such as Ginnie Mae and top-rated preferred corporate and municipal bonds.

7. Increase the percentage of FICA money that can go into such "privatized" funds annually, until eventually most of the retirement accounts are in the name of the individual taxpayer, and the money solely his or hers.

A similar system has been in effect in Chile since 1981. Taxpayers there get the choice of the government plan or one of twelve private plans, all insured by the government at a basic level. In the last decade the plans have earned 13 percent per year, guaranteeing a healthy retirement.

What will be the result of American's present plan?

If it continues as is, the baby boomers will be the grand suckers of the twenty-first century. If we change it—now—they'll be filling up the cruise ships that ply the world come the day they retire.

IX. Stop Illegal Immigration

The populist middle-class movement likes LEGAL immigration. It is the lifeblood of America, that which made us so different and once so much more successful than other nations.

Legal immigration should be encouraged, perhaps even expanded, and only amended to encourage more immigrants from Europe, who are openly discriminated against as the result of a 1965 change in the immigration law under the LBJ administration. (Prior to that, the immigration quota was based on the makeup of the then-current population of the nation.)

Legal immigrants should have the work and benefit rights of all Americans, though they should be screened more carefully to ensure that they will not be a burden on the people.

BUT ILLEGAL IMMIGRATION is destroying the sanctity and solvency of the nation, and must be stopped—cold—immediately. As several observers have pointed out, a nation with open borders has no sovereignty. America can hardly absorb every person in a deprived world who wants to gain the benefits of life here.

In simple terms, the middle class who pay the great bulk of the taxes, and whose jobs are in jeopardy, cannot afford it. Neither can the nation collectively, either economically or culturally.

There are two areas of easy entry to this country, and politicians, for all their patriotic bluster, are doing very little to control them. For a nation which won the Gulf War in a hundred hours, the inability to patrol our borders seems a sham, an activity that fails only because our politicians do not really care if it works or not.

One area is the nation's airports, where some 200,000 illegals arrive each year on tourist visas and never return home. The other is the porous Mexican border, where an estimated 1 to 2 million enter America each year after outwitting the hapless and undermanned Border Patrol.

Illegal Invasion

The invasion is so enormous that 80 percent of the children born in the San Diego County Hospital are the offspring of newly arrived illegals. These children are granted American citizenship and thus are immediately eligible for welfare—*which is a false interpretation of the Constitution*. In Los Angeles, 30 percent of the schoolchildren educated by taxpayers are illegals. The national cost of illegals? In dollars, some $15 billion a year.

In a cultural sense, it is creating two Americas—one traditional and the other Hispanic. Social Security, banks, corporations, even ATM machines now ask if you want to speak Spanish or English.

The welfare and social service rolls, as well as our prisons, are overloaded with illegals. If our welfare budget is strained for our own citizens, how can we handle the load of those who *illegally* seek a better life here?

Should we be heartless and turn them away? the unthinking ask.

The answer is simple. Why not show true compassion and ask the 300 million people in Latin America, and the one billion in India to join us within our borders?

The federal government, which has played a game with illegal immigration, states proudly that our deportation rate is *up* 25 percent. They fail to mention that for everyone deported, ten or more enter illegally.

This is a national problem of grave consequences and Congress and all our presidents for the past thirty years have been delinquent in protecting the country and its taxpayers.

The borders can be protected, but little will happen until the politicians feel the heat of an aroused citizenry.

X. The Corporation and More, Not Less, Jobs

The populist middle-class movement is pro-business, realizing that it is the engine of our prosperity.

BUT in the last decade, many workers—whether white collar or blue collar—have been hit with a triple whammy from the corporation, especially the large firms: Employees have had to face (1) the exporting of jobs overseas; (2) the computer revolution, which has made human beings less essential; (3) the downsizing of the American corporation.

Wall Street has zoomed, but most employees have done poorly, and the populist movement is not happy.

According to Challenger, Gray and Christmas, the Chicago "outplacement" organization which works with "downsized" management people to help them secure new jobs, corporations will let go another 500,000 people in 1996, mainly white collar and management personnel. (That's just the announced cuts.) Since 1989, when the downsizing went into full force, the tally of workers it has afflicted has passed 3.1 million.

In just one week in March 1996, more than 15,000 people were let go by corporations.

Some of the downsizing by corporations has been absolutely necessary. Witness IBM, which was on the fiscal rocks before Lou Gerstner reorganized to meet domestic and world competition—including the firing of sixty thousand people. Its stock has tripled since then.

Corporate Irresponsibility

But there's a fourth hit faced by employees. That is corporate irresponsibility, which treats American workers as if they are just numbers on a ledger. Almost every time a large firing is announced, the stock of the firm shoots up. The remaining executives become much richer as their stock options appreciate.

One wonders if all the downsizing is necessary or if some of it is just another manifestation of the greed that is making CEOs—the hired hands—much richer than their stockholders.

Salaries of $4, $5, even $10 and $15 million a year are becoming commonplace, creating a new class of executive that resembles more the Robber Barons of old than ordinary managers. In 1995, the compensation of CEOs increased by an average of 23 percent.

When interviewed, John Challenger explained that increasingly money market and mutual fund managers, who hold a large stock position in certain corporations, are sitting on the boards of these firms.

"They insist on a quick return on their investment," he explains. "They want the highest possible earnings each quarter so that the stock prices will keep rising and the earnings of their funds will go up as regularly—which is prudent action from their point of view. Often, after the company downsizes and eliminates workers and managers, the stock price rises. This may be good for the mutual funds, at least temporarily, but not necessarily for the corporation, or the nation. And surely not for the downsized employees."

Corporations can do great good or great harm to our

culture depending on their motives. If their total motivation is just to increase their quarterly bottom line and push up their stock prices and the valuc of their options, they will only contribute to the weakness of our nation. If, however, they can balance a healthy respect for the profit motive with one of social responsibility—by looking out for both the worker and the economy—they will be acting like good citizens.

Short-term goals, whether in politics or business, provide instant gratification, a failing which causes the downfall of governments and civilizations.

Corporations need to take heed and direct their energies into positive activity, not pure selfishness. If they do, fine. If not, the populist drive for fairness will somehow insist that they do.

Corporate Welfare

American corporations are not only too often poor corporate citizens, they also have their hands out.

Who fills them? Naturally, the taxpayers. One of the most egregious sins of Uncle Sam (and there are many as we've seen) is what has come to be known as "Corporate Welfare." That's big money from the U.S. Treasury that most Americans don't know about, and would cut off if they knew.

Steve Moore and Dean Stansel of the Cato Institute have done a study of the scam and have found that it costs us about $86 billion a year!

In all, Steve Moore estimates there are 127 federal subsidies to businesses!

The list includes special corporate tax breaks; subsidies for wholesale lumber from federal forests; federal roads to enable companies to take the lumber out; shaky and defaulted foreign loans by the Export-Import Bank that are picked up by taxpayers; drug company subsidies for manufacturing in Puerto Rico; low-interest money to the Rural Electrification Administration that is no longer needed; $333 million to car companies to help create new models (while they have $20 billion in the bank!); research money to such corporate fat cats as Texas Instruments, etc.

Outrageous!

Congress should not only cut out every penny of this unneeded welfare, but consider an Anti-Subsidy Act, which would make it illegal to appropriate money for any nongovernmental activity.

This would wipe out Corporate Welfare and most PORK in one fell swoop. A victory for beleaguered taxpayers.

XI. The "Fed" Should Lower Interest Rates

Every nation needs a central bank, but the Federal Reserve has become the target of a great deal of criticism, often rightly so.

The middle class needs cheap money in order for the nation to grow and for good jobs to be plentiful. Low interest rates also reduce the burden of personal debt, which is especially important today. America is increasingly a debtor nation, and families are heavily in hock to credit cards, home equity and mortgage loans.

But the Federal Reserve seems not to understand.

They have kept rates relatively, and artificially, high for most of the last six years. Chairman Alan Greenspan is generally a high interest man who fears inflation more than he wants a pro-growth economy. But he has guessed wrong several times. Inflation has been less of a problem than anyone thought, especially because of job insecurity and worker inability to demand increases in real wages.

The result has been a failure of true growth.

The nation has been hobbled needlessly. In 1990–91, both homeowners trying to sell their houses and builders knew that things were bad. But the Fed apparently didn't and kept rates high, pushing us into a recession. (Cynics say that they want rates as high as possible to protect the rich against wealth being downgraded by inflation.)

One argument against the behavior of the Fed is that they keep raising and lowering rates in a jerky roller-coaster manner that makes it impossible for the economy to operate steadily.

In 1994, for example, they suddenly changed course and lowered the rates, causing a miniboom as home-owners refinanced multibillions in home mortgages and were able to spend the savings. Then the Fed reversed itself again, and later in 1994, and in much of 1995, they raised interest rates *seven times*, creating a year of slow growth.

Change of Direction

Then, in late 1995, the Fed started to lower the rates again. Cynics once more point to a hidden motivation. In presidential election years, rates traditionally come down to make the incumbent, who has nominated the Fed chairman, look good—at least until after the election when rates often go back up.

Overall, this Fed has been a tight-money one. It shows in the nation's low-growth average, which is barely over 2 percent, not enough to create a vibrant economy. In the last quarter of 1995, growth was *only one-half of 1 percent*, a minirecession.

Bankers like low inflation even if it means a possible recession. But the middle class is willing to accept moderate inflation if it means growth, low interest rates and jobs. In fact, only a growth rate of 3.5 percent can balance the budget and solve the chronic, endemic, corrosive defects now present in the economy.

Who and what is the Federal Reserve?

It is run by a seven-person Board of Governors, appointed by the president and confirmed by the Senate. There are twelve completely private Federal Reserve district banks whose presidents also serve, on a rotating basis, on the Federal Reserve Open Market Committee.

The Board of Governors and five heads of the banks meet regularly to assess the state of the economy and to vote on keeping or changing the Fed Discount Rate and the so-called Fed Funds rate, two markers which dramatically affect the interest rates, helping to push them up or down.

Strong Critic

Mortimer Zuckerman, editor in chief of *U.S. News and World Report*, who has perhaps the sagest view of our Fed policy, is fearful that Mr. Greenspan has been too conservative, or "reactionary" as he calls it, in handling the economy.

In two recent editorials, he attacked the Federal Reserve's high-interest policy.

Pointing out in July 1995 that in May of that year 101,000 jobs "disappeared," Zuckerman commented: "The current slump is the handiwork of the Federal Reserve Board, an institution that is signally failing the nation. The Fed raised short-term interest rates seven times in roughly a year, doubling their levels and whacking the rate-sensitive industries such as housing and autos. Boom, the robust expansion of '94, has turned into the stagnation of mid-1995."

In February 1996, he sounded the alarm again.

Pointing out that Merrill Lynch was right in lowering its forecast of economic growth for 1996 down to less than 2 percent, he continued his attack on the performance of the Fed. "Short rates have come down too little and too late to boost a weakening economy," Zuckerman wrote. "The country does not have to endure the effects of the Fed's misjudgments in 1995 being extended into 1996."

Interest rates can make or break our economy. They can create jobs or destroy them. So far, the Fed has set a pattern of low growth, one which the middle class cannot afford.

We can blame Alan Greenspan and Company, but he's only the appointed official named by our politicians, specifically the President, and confirmed by still others, namely the Senate.

It is their ultimate responsibility, and once again they seem to be failing us.

In eleven major areas, we have seen that the system set up by professional politicians is not serving the mass of middle-class Americans.

The remedy is a peaceful but vocal revolution, one much deeper than that envisioned in the Contract with America. And surely different from the actions of the U.S. Congress over the last thirty years, an antipopulist record that has helped to shape the present MESS.

For the political parties, there's a lesson here. If either one hopes to become the majority party of the nation, they will have to first acknowledge that the people—and the failing economy—are not being served. Then they must adopt the populist platform, laid out carefully in the MIDDLE-CLASS MANIFESTO, from complete political reform to lower taxes to smaller government to better Social Security to immigration to low-interest rates.

From time to time (often insincerely), a handful of the points are covered by either one of the parties—but not enough to make an impact. In the long run, only those groups who follow these precepts will gain the loyalty of the people. It will surely take a major realignment within the two major parties, and failing that, the development of a strong third party.

Whatever the form the populist revolution takes, the people's voice will not be denied.

6

OUR UNETHICAL CONGRESS

"I Didn't Do Anything Wrong!"

Was the idea dreamed up by Speaker of the House Jim Wright of Texas clever?

Since there was a congressional ceiling on outside earnings except for book royalties, why not switch some outside income from honoraria to royalties?

Judge for yourself. Despite public indifference to his tome, he found ready customers. Lobbyists and other groups were quite willing to buy the book by the dozens to curry favor with the most powerful man in Congress.

The only hole in his scheme was that he set up an arrangement with the publisher in which he received unusually high royalties (55 percent rather than the usual

15) for the book, putting him closer to the ranks of the unethical than those of the literary giants.

When a Special Counsel was appointed to investigate this scheme and other infractions of the rules, Speaker Wright resigned, adding another chapter to the tales of unethical behavior that continue to dog members of the U.S. Congress.

This is not criminal activity. As we've seen, that is handled by the FBI and the Department of Justice. Unethical actions such as those of Speaker Wright are in violation of the rules of the House of Representatives, which, like the U.S. Senate, has an elaborate code of ethics. Those rules are *sometimes* enforced and other times winked at by sympathetic colleagues.

Separate Examination

The rules are so complex that the House publishes a 493-page "House Ethics Manual," which is almost as impenetrable as the IRS code. Since members of Congress are supposedly policed by their peers—or "self-policed" as they say—their behavior calls for a separate examination.

Despite their codes, unethical behavior continues in the august chambers of Congress. It covers the full spectrum of moral turpitude: from sweetheart business deals that are really disguised payoffs, to campaign finance violations, to failure to truthfully disclose assets and gifts, to overenthusiastic favors granted large contributors, to sexual misbehavior, to new excesses regularly conjured up by inventive legislators.

Are such violations important? Yes. Since Congress

makes the laws we all have to obey, the damage to democracy is enormous when they break their own rules.

With his royalty book scam, Jim Wright had exchanged a life of distinguished service to his country for a pittance. Why? What is there in the makeup of congressmen that makes risky bargains tempting for so many?

It seems to stem from an excess of greed in some, and extraordinary bad judgment in others.

Surely it's also born out of ambition and hubris, qualities that can upset an otherwise stable mind. Limelight seems to radiate rays that destroy character, especially among those in Congress.

Gingrich on the Firing Line

The man who had brought down Democratic Speaker Wright in 1989 was Republican backbencher Newt Gingrich, who is now the Speaker of the House and, like Wright, third in the line of succession for the presidency.

Gingrich himself has suddenly been thrust into the firing line. Democratic opponents have charged him with a number of infractions, all of which were investigated by the House Committee on Standards of Official Conduct (the House Ethics Committee).

Speaker Gingrich's troubles really began when he proudly, even brazenly, announced that he was to receive a $4.5 million advance on a book. It set off rocketlike signals of anger (and envy?) among the media and his colleagues, including several in his own party. Since it happened so soon after his elevation to the Speakership, it looked as if he were impatient, even desperate, to "cash in" on his new celebrityhood.

Six main charges were brought against Gingrich by Democrats salivating for revenge. In its report of December 12, 1995, the Ethics Committee, headed by Republican Nancy Johnson of Connecticut and made up of five House members from each party, voted unanimously to dismiss or take no action on five charges, while ordering an investigation on the sixth.

On the giant book advance, which Newt later defensively cut back to $1, he was exonerated with the comment that writing books was a congressional tradition.

(Senators Gary Hart of Colorado and William Cohen of Maine, for instance, had collaborated on a novel, and Newt himself had "written" a fiction potboiler in 1995 that is best forgotten. One side effect of the Gingrich controversy was that the House Ethics Committee has proposed a law limiting income from book authorship to $20,000, the ceiling on all outside income.)

While most charges were dismissed, the committee did note that Gingrich had broken House Rule 45 by allowing a personal friend to interview employees for the Speaker's office. The committee also ruled that he had improperly given out an "800" number on the floor of the House to promote his college course, Renewing American Civilization. But no action was taken.

The big brouhaha involved his college course, which has brought Gingrich some intellectual attention and even spawned cassettes and a newspaper. The Ethics Committee has not cleared Gingrich on one charge: that he "misused entities" such as the nonprofit Kennesaw State

College Foundation and the Progress and Freedom Foundation to help support his teaching.

The inference is that he may have violated section 501(c)(3) of the United States codes which regulate non-profit organizations, in raising money for political rather than educational purposes. The House committee has appointed a Special Counsel, James M. Cole, a Washington attorney, to investigate. The danger to Gingrich is that Special Counsels, like Kenneth Starr on Whitewater, have a tendency to broaden their inquiries.

In February 1996, Judge Louis Oberdorfer dismissed a suit by the FEC against GOPAC, the speaker's PAC.

Partisan Fire

The charges against Gingrich may have been tit for tat to avenge Jim Wright. A new charge (tat for tit?) has been leveled by Republicans in the House Ethics Committee against the chief Democrat in the house, Dick Gephardt, the minority leader. This one involves personal gain and false statements, as do many other lapses in ethics.

Representative Jennifer Dunn, a Washington State Republican, charges that Gephardt misled both Congress and the IRS about a real estate deal. She claims that Gephardt has avoided capital gains taxes involving his $700,000 beach house in North Carolina.

The original impetus for the charge came from an exposé on Gephardt in *Insight* magazine written by Paul Rodriguez, the journalist who helped break the House banking scandal. Dunn's office spent months following it up before she filed charges on February 2, 1996.

In the 1980s, Gephardt bought a condo on North

Carolina's Outer Banks and then in 1991 exchanged it in a tax-free swap for a vacant piece of land in a nearby exclusive resort called Corolla Light. By swapping it instead of selling the condo and buying the land, he saved $17,680 in capital gains tax. It was all legal *if* the statements made to the IRS were true.

In 1992, Gephardt sold a half interest in the lot to an insurance broker and his wife, then obtained a $493,100 loan to build a large six-bedroom house on the lot. To gain their mortgage with a smaller down payment and lower interest, the Gephardts pledged that it was to be their own home, and not a rental property. In fact, both Gephardts initialed a notation that the property was to be used "only as a second home."

BUT, says Congresswoman Dunn, Gephardt went ahead and rented it, taking in between $15,000 and $50,000. In early 1994, he refinanced the loan with the same pledge not to rent out the house.

The seven-page complaint against Gephardt makes the following four charges:

1. In his financial disclosure to Congress, he called what is the "Duck Property" in North Carolina a "secondary residence." But to qualify for a tax-free exchange with the IRS, he characterized it as being held for investment, or rental, purposes. Therefore, says Ms. Dunn, Gephardt is guilty of violating either the IRS code or the Ethics in Government Act.

2. In his financial disclosure of 1992, Gephardt characterized the second property, so-called Corolla Light Property, as being for investment purposes only. But to close a loan to build on it, he called it a secondary home for his personal use. So, claims Ms. Dunn, he either violated the Ethics in Government law or made a false statement to the bank, which could be a federal crime.

3. In 1992–94, he failed to disclose personal debts totaling $66,000, which violates the Ethics in Government Act.

4. Experienced fund-raiser Gephardt claimed fund-raising expenses of $70,000 in the North Carolina area but surprisingly took in almost no proceeds. The money was ostensibly spent on catering and lodging with companies owned by the man who loaned Gephardt the money to buy the Corolla Light property in the first place.

(Mr. Gephardt's spokeswoman called the complaint "a rehash of old and discredited allegations.")

The matter, like Gingrich's, is in the hands of the House Ethics Committee.

Hanky-Panky

The ethics debate revolving around these men at the top of the legislative pyramid echoes the public's feeling that there's too much hanky-panky on both sides of the aisle. Even if not criminal, the unethical actions of our congressmen have unnerved a constituency already worried about the sanctity of their government.

Why is all this happening? Is it because the proximity to power pushes public officials over into moral lapses? Or because individuals with poor character are attracted to the game of politics in the first place?

It's probably some of each—that we are dealing with certain flawed personalities who are then pressed by the temptations of power and celebrity.

Some of the unethical behavior in Congress rotates around campaign funds. They can involve mere technicalities of the law or small fortunes. The latter was the case in 1995 with Enid Waldholtz, Republican congresswoman from Utah, whose tangled campaign finances have yet to be fully untangled.

The first clues were inconsistencies in her reports to the Federal Elections Commission (FEC). Part of the problem seemed to involve her husband, Joe Waldholtz, the treasurer of her winning 1994 campaign. By August 1994, she had raised only $280,000 and was trailing in the polls in a three-way race.

Then, suddenly, a small fortune was pumped into her campaign fund. First, she put in $880,000, then less than two weeks before the election, she added $650,000 more—all supposedly her own money.

In all, more than $1.8 million went into her campaign account. If she had raised that from PACs and $1,000 contributions from individuals it was legal. Or if it were truly her own money, it was also strangely ethical as well. (As we've seen, the eccentric campaign law, supported by a 1976 Supreme Court decision, allows the rich to swamp other candidates by spending *any* amount of their money, or half the money held jointly with a spouse.)

But where would the Waldholtzes, who were known to have numerous debts, come up with such a small fortune?

The answer was allegedly daddy. Mrs. Waldholtz's father, a former member of the Pacific Coast Stock Exchange, reportedly lent the money to the couple to pay off their numerous debts. But the cash allegedly wended its way into her campaign fund and was unreported to the FEC as her own—which is illegal. The case blew up on November 11, 1995, when Joe Waldholtz vanished, then later turned himself in to the Justice Department.

In an attempt to clear her name, Congresswoman Waldholtz held that now famous five-hour marathon press conference in Salt Lake City. Punctuating her copious tears with her protestations of innocence, she blamed it all on her husband.

A spokesperson for Congresswoman Waldholtz said that she hadn't even read the false FEC statement. Supposedly, her husband told her she was a rich woman because of his multimillion dollar gift to her, which was an invention. Her plea? She was totally ignorant of how much money she had, or where it went, or how it got into her campaign fund—hardly a testimonial to the intelligence or veracity of a member of Congress. In March, she announced that she wouldn't run for reelection.

Mrs. Waldholtz's case is in the hands of the Ethics Committee and the FEC. Joe Waldholtz will have to deal with the Department of Justice.

Flexible Ethics

There is a feeling among critics that members of Congress are too soft on each other, and there's some evidence to back the complaint. Gary Ruskin, head of the nonprofit Congressional Accountability Project, a Ralph Nader group, is adamant that when it comes to politicians overseeing politicians, there's a great deal of friendly winking and permissiveness.

"The ethics committees in Congress are more of a system to protect their fellow members rather than to protect the public," he says. "Too often they respond to serious unethical behavior with merely a slap on the wrist, or nothing at all."

A case that supports this complaint is that of Senator Mark Hatfield of Oregon, who was charged with accepting gifts and not disclosing them as the Senate required. The charge was particularly important because Hatfield is now chairman of the *molto* powerful Senate Appropriations Committee, a post he also held from 1981 to 1986, when the unethical behavior took place.

Did it involve items of little significance, too petty to influence a man of his power?

In one case it did—a gift of a $400 compact disc player. But that was just the tip of an inventory of goodies Hatfield had secretly taken. The full list of gifts released by the Senate Ethics Committee confirms the old saw about politicians: "He's on the take."

The unreported gifts to the senator included:

- A Steuben glass cross, valued at $3,875
- $17,000 in home improvement costs to remodel and expand his bedroom
- A Boehm Carolina Wren, value $725
- A Steuben glass eagle, $535
- The forgiveness of $4,415 interest due on loans
- A framed Audubon wild turkey print, $3,336
- Two signet rings, valued at $5,500
- The forgiveness of $5,005 interest due on loans
- A bronze beaver sculpture, $2,100

- Reimbursement of travel expenses by the University of South Carolina, 1985, 1986, and 1987
- The disc player

The loot came as gifts from six different sources, but Hatfield's major patron was Dr. James B. Holderman, former president of the University of South Carolina. Hatfield had a close relationship with Holderman, including an official one involving federal appropriations to the college, which Hatfield's committee controlled.

Slap on Wrist

Did Hatfield go to jail for bribery? Did he get expelled from the Senate? Did he lose his chairmanship?

Nothing of the sort. He was "rebuked" by the Senate, a form of censure not unlike sending an obstreperous teenager to his room where he can listen to his new stereo CD. After that slap on the wrist, Hatfield merely went about his business, and was even twice reelected.

The Ethics Committee acknowledged that Hatfield handled "routine official actions" involving the university, but found that there was "no linkage" between the gifts and his Senate actions on behalf of the school. Their conclusion is of course highly unlikely and sounds much like friendly cover for a fellow pol.

Another weak (or nonexistent) response to a complaint involved Phil Gramm of Texas. "Senator Phil Gramm has a charmed way with the Senate Ethics Committee," the *New York Times* commented in a 1994 editorial.

The gist of the *Times*'s argument was that Gramm "had used taxpayer money for campaign expenses and to fund personal travel with his wife and sons." In his case, the Ethics Committee "does not bother to investigate," lamented the *Times*. "It simply accepts his version of the events, provided in secret correspondence, and then quietly issues a letter that the Senator can use to deflect critics."

The editorial also commented on a previous tussle in which Gramm escaped a reprimand. A builder who also operated three troubled S&Ls spent $117,000 to complete a waterfront house for Gramm in rural Maryland. Gramm paid only $63,433 to the builder and S&L operator, on whose behalf the senator had contacted federal regulators.

"Senators Howell Heflin and Warren Rudman, then chairman and vice chairman of the ethics committee," said the *Times*, "hastily gave Mr. Gramm a letter declaring that the builder's hefty contribution to the Senator's home was merely a cost overrun and not a 'gift' under Senate rules."

New York Republican Senator Alfonse D'Amato has also had a brush with the Ethics Committee, and got off with a wrist slap.

A complaint was filed against him by Democrat Mark Green, who had been beaten by D'Amato in the race for the Senate. The major charges were fourfold.

1. That in 1985 the senator had promised to introduce legislation to restrict "junk bonds" but failed to do so after Drexel Burnham Lambert, which

specialized in these bonds, made substantial contributions to his campaign.

2. That D'Amato engaged in improper conduct in connection with HUD's S235 mortgage subsidy program in Island Park, Long Island, his hometown. He was alleged to have interfered in the program by using his position in order to obtain inexpensive, government-subsidized homes for two of his cousins.
3. That he also engaged in improper conduct in regard to HUD projects in Puerto Rico. When the HUD scandal broke in the late 1980s, it was learned that the island commonwealth had received seven times its "fair share" of HUD rehabilitation money. D'Amato was accused of lobbying HUD on behalf of Puerto Rican developers in return for contributions.
4. That Unisys (formerly Sperry), a large defense contractor on Long Island at the time, had hired the senator's brother, Armand D'Amato, to advance their cause. The senator was charged with allowing his brother to use his office to write official letters to the Defense Department on behalf of Unisys.

In addition, there were twelve other charges, ranging from contracts to redevelop public housing in White Plains, the Roosevelt Raceway, a HUD grant for a drug rehab center proposed by black ministers led by Al Sharpton.

A Special Counsel, Henry F. Schuelke III, was

named to investigate D'Amato. Forty-one taped telephone intercepts were made of persons other than the senator, and fifty-six witnesses were deposed. Of these, twenty-five refused to testify and took the Fifth Amendment. Ten other witnesses said that if called, they would also refuse to testify on the grounds that it might incriminate them.

On August 2, 1991, the Senate Ethics Committee delivered its decision.

On the Drexel Burnham Lambert matter, the committee found that there was no evidence to support the charge. In regard to favoritism on the subsidized homes in Island Park, the committee found "that there is insufficient credible evidence to provide substantial cause to conclude that a violation within the committee's jurisdiction has occurred."

On the HUD/Puerto Rico matter, the committee reported that they were "disadvantaged by the unavailability of several essential witnesses who have asserted their constitutional privilege against self-incrimination." They decided that there was "insufficient credible evidence" and that "further proceedings" could not be pursued at the time.

On the question of his brother using the senator's office to advance the cause of Unisys, the committee did find against Senator D'Amato, stating that "Senator D'Amato conducted the business of his office in an improper and inappropriate manner," and that he was "negligent in failing to establish appropriate standards."

In regard to the twelve additional charges, D'Amato was cleared of them all, and as everyone knows, he is now the chairman of the Senate Banking Committee.

Occasional Crackdown

Both the House and the Senate Ethics Committees often seem controlled by whim or blatant favoritism. But they *can* be tough on errant congressmen. Such was the case with Senator David F. Durenberger of Minnesota, who used a twist on the Wright book deal to pump up his income.

Before the massive pay raise of 1991, which has brought the base salary up to $133,600, senators were allowed to receive "honoraria" for making speeches, but there was a strict limit on the total amount they could receive.

Durenberger concocted a scheme to get around the Senate rule. In fact, he was so pleased with himself that he mentioned his plan to other senators, assuming it would wash—which, of course, it couldn't.

What Durenberger did was ingenious, if quite unethical. He made an arrangement with a publisher to print books he had written, then traveled around, making 113 "promotional lectures," supposedly for his books.

Instead of giving honoraria, which was the usual practice, Durenberger's hosts paid the publisher a substantial amount for his speeches. The publisher then gave Durenberger a "stipend"—not a limited "honorarium"—for his work.

It was not an insignificant scam. The stipend was $100,000 a year, paid quarterly. As the Senate Select Committee on Ethics pointed out, Durenberger often didn't even "promote" the books, or if he did, it was only in passing. On one occasion, he received a $5,000 check made out to "Durenberger for the U.S. Senate," which went into the book account, then back to him personally.

The senator had a second scheme going. It granted him $65 a day in expenses from the Senate for staying in his own condo in Minneapolis! He arranged to sell a half-interest in the apartment, making it appear not to be his, then billed the Senate for his stays.

After an investigation, the Senate Ethics Committee "denounced" the senator and ordered him to reimburse the government $29,050 with interest, plus give an additional $93,730 to charity. He wasn't expelled, but after his term expired, he left the Senate.

Hushed Up

For every exposé of an unethical practice, like that of Durenberger or Wright or Hatfield, there are others that are unknown or, if known to Congress, carefully hushed up. But sometimes they surface and offer the public a clear view of the unethical underside of the U.S. Congress.

That was the case with Senator Robert Packwood. Known to some as a womanizer who tried to kiss and grab women within easy flirting distance, he also had his bouts with heavy drinking. But otherwise he was considered not only a knowledgeable senator, particularly on finance, but someone who was highly ethical when it came to government business.

Then the truth came out. It had been buried all the time in his private diary, an eight-hundred-page document in which he had chronicled his life over the years. To find evidence of his sexual misconduct, the diary was subpoenaed by the Senate. To their amazement, a whole other Packwood came out of the pages, offering a secret insight into what can and does go on in the august body.

The Ethics Committee report is filled with details of Packwood's sexual crudity, some of which reads like romance fiction:

> Ms. . . . tried to get around the Senator and out of the office. . . . Finally he grabbed her; when she tried to kick him in the shins, he stood on her feet. He grabbed her ponytail with his left hand, pulled her head back forcefully, and gave her a big wet kiss with his tongue in her mouth. She did not taste or smell any alcohol. With his right hand, he reached up under her skirt and grabbed the edge of her panty girdle and tried to pull it down. She struggled, got away from him, and ran into the front office. He stalked out past her, paused at the threshold to the hallway, and told her, "If not today, then someday," and left.

But as it turned out, his political shenanigans were even more shocking. One charge leveled against Packwood was that he altered entries in his diary *after* it was subpoenaed by the Ethics Committee. This angered his colleagues, helping to trigger his expulsion from the Senate.

Candid Confession

On March 20, 1992, Packwood confessed to his diary about what sounds like a blatantly unethical deal.

> Elaine has been talking to me privately about independent expenditures. Apparently the Automobile

> Dealers are willing to do some spending against AuCoin [his opponent in the Senate race]. Of course we can't do anything about it . . . going to do it. We've got to destroy any evidence that we've ever had . . . so that we have no connection with any independent expenditure.

This is a reference to the 24E exemption in the campaign finance law, which has no ceiling on the amount an independent person or group can spend for a candidate—as long as he has absolutely no connection with them.

Knowing that his confession was a faux pas, Packwood cleaned up the diary entry. The rewrite reflected the soul of innocence. "We want independent expenditures to be truly independent," he now wrote with perfect hindsight.

Packwood became a regular revisionist of his own history. One of his most dramatic rewrites involved a fellow senator, and a conversation which he thought might constitute "a felony."

The dialogue in the diary was between Packwood and Senator Phil Gramm, whom the Ethics Committee report called "Senator X" in order to protect his privacy.

The original entry seemed incriminating: "Senator Gramm again promised $100,000 for Party-building activities. And what was said in that room would be enough to convict us all of something," Packwood initially wrote. "He [Gramm] says, now, of course you know there can't be any legal connection between this money and Senator Packwood, but we know that it'll be used for his benefit. . . . God, there's Elaine and I sitting there. I think that's a felony. I'm not sure. This is an area of the law I don't want to know. Senator Gramm left. Elaine and I headed back to the motel."

In his rewritten version, the unethical gist of the conversation had vanished. When questioned about the alteration by the Ethics Committee, Packwood became creative. He first claimed that he had been wrong in his evaluation of Gramm's comment and then that it was surely all in jest. He then also claimed that the original conversation recorded in his diary had never even taken place! Someone in Senator Gramm's position, Packwood insisted, would never take that kind of risk.

Invention, reinvention, gospel or what?

Abysmal Record

We have already looked at the congressional record of crimes committed and prosecuted. Unfortunately, the record of unethical behavior is equally disheartening.

In 1992, the House Ethics Committee issued a document summarizing cases going back to 1798. There are a total of seventy-one cases in which they found unethical behavior, the great majority having taken place since 1967. At that time, Congressman Adam Clayton Powell of New York City used official money for personal travel and paid his wife a federal salary.

In the early days of the Republic, there was a case in which one House member hit another with a cane and the victim retaliated with fireplace tongs. In another (1838) one congressman killed another in a duel over angry words spoken in a floor debate. (They recommended he be expelled, but nothing was done.)

In 1857, three House members from New York and one from Connecticut were accused of accepting bribes. One was excused for lack of evidence and the other three resigned. In 1870, Representative Benjamin F. Whittemore of South Carolina was accused of selling appointments to West Point and Annapolis, and resigned.

Naturally, there were charges leveled against congressmen in the years following, but it wasn't until the last two decades that unethical behavior in the House and Senate became quite common—or was more closely watched.

The cases cover a near-infinite variety, illustrating that there is no behavior congressmen deem beneath them.

Members have been charged with:

- Filing false financial statements
- Soliciting campaign money from staffers
- Taking free flights on corporate aircraft (Wouldn't they have to censure half of Congress?)
- Borrowing from campaign funds
- Intervening on behalf of an S&L in which the member had a financial interest
- Helping a member's wife get legal fees from a defense contractor
- Using campaign funds for personal purposes
- Allowing another member to cast his vote
- Taking illegal gratuities
- Authorizing salary disbursements to ghost employees, then keeping the money
- Negotiating a loan from proceeds of narcotics sales

- Simple bribery
- The massive abuse of check cashing privileges—the great House Banking scandal of 1992

Here is a sampling, some of which were recorded by the congressional ethics committee and others of which were detailed in a study by *Roll Call*, a newspaper covering activities on the Hill:

In 1976, Representative William Clay (D., Missouri) was sued by the Justice Department for violating the False Claims Act by submitting fake travel vouchers to the House. The case was dropped when he agreed to repay the House $1,754.

In 1983, Representative Louis Stokes (D., Ohio), who had served two terms as chairman of the House Ethics Committee, was arrested for drunk driving, convicted on a lesser charge and paid a $250 fine.

Representative Gerry Studds (D., Massachusetts), one of the three acknowledged homosexuals in the House, was censured in 1983 for having sex with a seventeen-year-old male page. He was reelected the next year with a 56 percent vote.

In 1984, Representative Geraldine Ferraro (D., New York), who was the Democratic nominee for vice president under Walter Mondale, was investigated by the House Ethics Committee for failure to disclose business interests of her husband, John Zaccaro.

She held a press conference on August 21 and released documents detailing her finances. She said that she and her husband would be sending a check for $53,000 to the Internal Revenue Service for an underpayment error dating back six years. On December 3, 1984, after she and Mondale had lost the election and she was no longer a member of the House, the committee issued a statement that Ms. Ferraro had committed ten violations of the House disclosure laws.

In 1985, Senator Bob Kasten (R., Wisconsin) was arrested on drunk driving charges and agreed to enter an alcohol abuse course.

In 1986, Representative James Weaver (D., Oregon) was brought before the Ethics Committee because he had lost $113,169 of his campaign committee's money speculating in the commodities market between 1981 and 1983. He claimed he took the funds in repayment of money he had lent the campaign. The committee ruled he had used campaign money for personal uses, but took no further action because he had reported it on his FEC form.

Also in 1986, Representative W. C. Daniel (R., Virginia) was found by the Ethics Committee to have accepted sixty-eight free flights from the Beech Aircraft Company over a period of eight years. On nineteen occasions, said the committee, he had also submitted "erroneous" vouchers for auto travel. When Daniel reimbursed Beech and the government, the committee decided to take no action.

In 1987, Representative Mary Rose Oakar (D., Ohio) was probed by the House Ethics Committee on charges that she had kept an employee on her payroll for two years even though the aide had moved to New York. She repaid the money and the Ethics Committee took no formal action.

In 1988, Representative Jim Bates (D., California) was issued a "letter of reproval" by the Ethics Committee for improperly using congressional aides to do campaign work. He was also accused of sexually harassing female aides. Admitting his transgressions, he underwent sensitivity training.

In 1989, Representative Tony Coelho (D., California), the majority whip who aspired to become speaker, resigned in the wake of revelations about his profitable junk bond investment arranged by an S&L owner and the brokerage house Drexel Burnham Lambert. When he faced an Ethics Committee probe, he quickly resigned.

That same year, after a two-year investigation, Representative Charles Rose (D., North Carolina) was issued a letter of reproval by the House Ethics Committee for using more than $60,000 in campaign funds for personal purposes over a period of seven years.

In 1989, Representative Donald Lukens (R., Ohio) was convicted of contributing to the delinquency of a minor by having sex with a sixteen-year-old girl. He was sentenced to thirty days in jail. After his conviction, he was accused of fondling a Capitol elevator operator and asking her to have sex with him. Facing an Ethics Committee hearing, he resigned from the House.

In 1990, saying "I should have known better," Representative Barney Frank (D., Massachusetts), an open homosexual, was reprimanded by a 408 to 18 vote for fixing the parking tickets of a male prostitute and making misleading statements to parole officers on the prostitute's behalf. Both an expulsion and a censure motion were defeated, and he was merely "reprimanded." Frank was reelected with a two-thirds majority soon after.

The Keating Five

Perhaps the most highly publicized ethics case in the recent history of the U.S. Congress was the so-called Keating Five investigation, which involved five senators, including four Democrats and one Republican, and alleged favors for contributions.

It revolved around the Lincoln Savings and Loan Association scam, which cost taxpayers *$2 billion* when the Phoenix, Arizona, institution collapsed in the S&L debacle of the late 1980s.

The vortex of the scandal was the owner of Lincoln, Charles H. Keating, Jr., an extravagant contributor (as it turned out, with taxpayer money!) to a number of politicians, especially five senators—John Glenn (D., Ohio), John McCain (R., Arizona), Dennis DeConcini (D., Arizona), Donald Riegle (D., Michigan), and Alan Cranston (D., California).

Keating, who was finally jailed for bank fraud, was asked if he expected that his generosity would gain him influence with the senators.

"I would certainly hope so," he responded in a now-classic answer.

Keating spread his largesse around massively. He raised $994,000 for organizations closely affiliated with Senator Cranston, and gave $49,000 to Cranston's 1984 presidential bid and his 1986 senatorial campaign. In addition, Keating gave $85,000 to the California Democratic Party, along with a $300,000 line of credit.

Keating contributed $31,000 to DeConcini's 1982 campaign and another $54,000 to his reelection bid.

Senator John Glenn received $200,000 from Keating's corporate fund for the nonfederal account of Glenn's multicandidate PAC. In addition, Keating, his associates and friends contributed $24,000 to Glenn's senatorial campaign and $18,200 for his presidential bid in 1984.

Senator John McCain received $56,000 from Keating and associates for his two House races, then $54,000 for his Senate contest. McCain and family rode on Keating's corporate plane and took commercial flights paid for by Keating, travel worth $13,433. (McCain ultimately reimbursed Keating.) He and his family also vacationed with Keating in the Bahamas for four consecutive years, at a home provided by the banker.

Senator Riegle was also the beneficiary (or victim?) of Keating's free-wheeling support of American politicians. In 1987, at the Ponchartrain Hotel in Detroit, which was owned by Keating's company, Keating et al. raised $78,250 for Riegle's reelection fund.

Rally Round the Contributor

Keating ran into trouble when the Federal Home Loan Bank Board (FHLBB) began looking for improprieties in Lincoln's affairs. His first response was to ask his powerful friends to come to the rescue. He was not disappointed. All five, to varying degrees, rallied to his cause.

Was it unethical? What can a congressman do to help a constituent? What about a big contributor who's not a constituent? Could a senator do anything to help Keating and still act ethically?

The whole debate has a kind of metaphysical or Talmudic ring to it. The reason, of course, is that there are no clear cut answers when MONEY pushes its ugly head into the equation, and politicians' minds are twisted by the lure of large contributions.

That obviously happened in the Keating adventure, as it does hundreds of times each year in Congress.

Keating complained to the five senators that the FHLBB, which was investigating his S&L, was being unfair. On April 2, 1987, four of them met in Washington with FHLBB officials to ask about their examination of Lincoln S&L. They were told that it was in the hands of the San Francisco office. A week later, all five senators met with four officials of that local office, and learned that a criminal referral against Keating was in the works.

After these two meetings, McCain and Riegle took no further action on behalf of Keating. But in January 1988, ten months later, Senator Glenn arranged a luncheon for Keating with Speaker of the House Jim Wright. Then, between February and April, Senator DeConcini made several calls asking the FHLBB to promptly consider Keating's application to sell Lincoln, apparently before it came crashing down, as it finally did.

Senator Cranston was the most active of the five. He set up two meetings between Keating and M. Danny Wall, the chairman of the FHLBB, then followed up with phone calls to Wall on behalf of Keating. Cranston also called other members of the board and other regulatory officials on behalf of his monied patron.

The Ethics Committee appointed a Special Counsel, Robert S. Bennett, to investigate, and on November 20, 1991, they issued their report. It used a variety of adjectives to describe the action of four of the senators, from too "aggressive" in pursuing Keating's cause, to "improper" to "poor judgment" to "inappropriate" to "insensitivity." But no action was taken against the four.

Cranston Is Target

The committee's fire was saved for Cranston, who they found not only had numerous meetings with Keating but had made *thirteen* contacts with federal regulators on the S&L operator's behalf.

"There is clear and convincing evidence before the committee," they wrote, "showing that Senator Cranston solicited and received contributions from Mr. Keating in a manner which linked the contributions from Mr. Keating with official action."

Their own action? They wrote that they "hereby strongly and severely reprimand Senator Alan Cranston." They also noted that he was in poor health and did not intend to seek reelection.

What does it prove? That Cranston and the others were especially naughty? Perhaps, or perhaps not. In some ways, their actions were relatively routine for members of Congress. The difference was that their interventions involved a very rich patron who went to jail. The case was highly publicized and the unethical behavior was less well disguised. Most important, they got caught.

(There is a pitiful, almost tragic, aspect to this and similar cases in Congress, a kind of whoredom practiced by men who should instead be at the moral height of their careers. But as long as money creates access, this will continue to go on. One former senator, Rudy Boschwitz of Minnesota, even formalized the game. He gave out blue stamps for $1,000 contributions, then instructed his staff to bring the blue-stamped letters directly to him!)

How do complaints come before the Ethics Committees? How does one bring charges against a member of Congress?

Besides the uneven hand of justice shown by the committees, it's all based on a flawed system. Congress does no investigating on its own and merely waits for someone to accuse someone else. There are now two ways to initiate cases. First, members can complain about unethical behavior of their peers, which almost always involves partisan backbiting, even when the case has merit.

Democrats snitch on Republicans; Republicans file charges against Democrats.

This is crude, but it does sometimes turn the adversarial stance of the two parties into something positive for taxpayers. In fact, most exposés come out of partisanship. Would Republicans have pursued Watergate and uncovered Nixon's cover-up? Would Democrats have tried to unearth the sleaze of Whitewater? Obviously not.

Better Way

There is a second and better method, which operates in lieu of an intelligent official policy. Many complaints come through public service groups such as Ralph Nader's Congressional Accountability Project and the Common Cause Organization, both of which do good work.

(Charges made by Common Cause range over both parties, but Nader's group seems to be more partisan, putting more energy into pursuing Republicans, who account for eight of their ten complaints to the Ethics Committees. They deny it, calling it a statistical coincidence.)

Then what is the answer to initiating charges?

The Nader group feels that Special Counsels should be in charge of each investigation, which makes good sense. However, I believe the public must go beyond that to protect the sanctity of the U.S. Congress, whose reputation for honesty is deservedly poor, and whose Ethics Committees are far from aggressive in disciplining its members.

My plan is simple:

WE MUST ESTABLISH AN INDEPENDENT NONPARTISAN OMBUDSMAN GROUP TO TAKE OVER MOST OF THE INVESTIGATIVE WORK OF THE ETHICS COMMITTEES IN BOTH HOUSES OF CONGRESS. THE OMBUDSMEN WILL DEAL WITH COMPLAINTS FROM OTHER MEMBERS, STAFF AND THE PUBLIC, BUT WILL ALSO INVESTIGATE ON THEIR OWN ON A CONTINUOUS BASIS.

If they find anything of significance, they will issue an immediate report to the media. *After that,* the Ethics Committees will act as judges and issue their decision. Infringements that are not criminal will be treated with a rebuke and a warning. *But on the second infringement of ethics rules, the member will automatically be expelled from Congress.*

The ethical problem in Congress today is buttressed

by secrecy. Ethics Committees will say absolutely nothing unless and until they issue a final report. Most errant behavior by members is unknown, and staff surely won't snitch on their bosses. We need open government, and only official watchdogs can provide it.

As we've seen, the system is implicitly flawed because of the power of money, something we hope to correct in Chapter 8. But there's also a pampering of members of Congress that makes them feel separate from and superior to the rest of the nation.

Perks and Privilege

Strict term limits will help solve the *übermenschen* syndrome, but there's another overriding fault in the system: the overgenerous perks and pensions granted members of Congress. Public pressure has reduced such privileges as check-kiting and the House bank, and members now have to obey the laws they pass for others. But privilege is still rampant, as a report from Gordon S. Jones, president of the Association of Concerned Taxpayers, dramatically shows.

Perks sustain the sense that members of Congress are more privileged and important than you and me. Here, then, is a checklist:

1. Despite a giant pay increase, members still get a special untalked-about $3,000 housing deduction off their federal income taxes!
2. The IRS does for them what they won't do for you. At tax time, IRS personnel set up shop in

each House and Senate office building to help members and staff fill out their taxes.

3. They pay no D.C. sales taxes on items purchased in the Capitol building.
4. Even if they live in the District of Columbia, they (and two of their top staffers) are exempt from paying the especially high D.C. income taxes.
5. The National Gallery lends original paintings to members to decorate their offices.
6. There's a special office to wrap packages, free of charge, for members and senior staffers.
7. Both the House and the Senate have a staff of photographers who take pictures of members and constituents, then send them out, all free of charge.
8. They have a free parking space at National and Dulles airports, just steps away from the terminal. Regular citizens have to lug their bags from a paid public parking space.
9. Special shops in House and Senate buildings frame pictures—from ordinary snapshots to huge posters—for members at no cost.
10. On defeat or retirement, members are allowed to take their taxpayer-paid-for desk and chair home as souvenirs at a ridiculously low fee.
11. Stationery stores in the basement of the House and Senate offer super-discount gifts, cassettes, stationery, etcetera to members and staff—at a cost of a $1 million subsidy by taxpayers.
12. Members and staff fly around the country, and

back and forth to their homes, on government-paid airline tickets. Executive branch employees can't keep the frequent-flyer miles for themselves, but members and staff in Congress can—providing taxpayer-paid free private trips.

13. When members and staff use their personal cars for business, they are reimbursed at a higher mileage rate than we taxpayers can claim on our IRS rcturns.

14. Seventy-nine senators with the longest seniority each get a "hideway" office off the Senate floor and Capitol hallways. This is in addition to their regular offices.

15. Long-distance phone services are available free of charge to members and their senior staffs. At home, they can tap into it with a special code.

16. The Library of Congress operates a lending library service for members and staff. There are no fines for overdue books and every year thousands of books go unreturned.

17. Members have numerous opportunities for patronage, including the nomination and selection of young pages, a choice job they can hand out to children of friends.

18. Leaders in the House and Senate are provided with free limos along with chauffeurs, most of whom are Capitol police taken away from their regular duties to drive congressional brass.

19. The House and Senate operate a special radio and television studio where members can make tapes, free of charge, then send them out to stations in their district to advance their cause, even for reelection.

No single one of these perks is overwhelming in itself. But collectively they create a culture of privilege that helps to insulate members and their staffs from the normal day-to-day activity of most Americans, the people they're supposed to represent.

Retirement Perk

One major perk that is outlandish is their gold-plated retirement pensions. Members of Congress who began before 1984 have a pension system that is unparalleled in its generosity—*with our money.*

We've seen that Tom Foley left with a $123,000-a-year pension, which means that some $3 million will be coming to him over his normal life expectancy. Of those members retiring at the end of 1996, one will be receiving over $100,000 a year beginning in January 1997, and ten more will receive pensions larger than their salary of $89,500 before the huge 1991 raise.

The National Taxpayers Union has created a chart of retiring members and it includes some sinus-clearing figures. Congresswoman Pat Schroeder of Colorado, for instance, is only fifty-six years old, so her beginning pension is a touch smaller—$74,915. BUT because her remaining life expectancy is twenty-nine years, the expected cost of her retirement is $4,182,573!

How did these pensions get so high? Quite simple. Most of the congressmen who came in before 1984 put 8 percent of their salary in the retirement system. But taxpayers add *almost five dollars for every one* of theirs, what's called a "defined benefit" plan.

Second, the size of congressional retirement pensions is figured from the three highest years of salary. When members got their enormous pay raise, their pensions jumped accordingly.

To protect them from inflation, members even enjoy a COLA, an annual cost-of-living increase to their pensions, something 90 percent of private retirement plans cannot boast. Within a matter of a decade or less, many members will receive a pension check larger than their former salary.

What should we do about this excess?

Well, when (and if) term limits are operative, and the days of professional politicians are over, members of Congress will not need—*and should not receive*—formal retirement pensions. A 401-K plan in which the government might match up to 5 percent of their salaries on a 50 percent ratio will be quite sufficient. They can then move their 401-K to their next job. (Most ex-congressmen have no trouble gaining employment, especially as lobbyists—see Chapter 7.)

How much will the taxpayer save?

Just among the forty-five departing incumbents in 1996, the saving would be an estimated $81 million. But more important is the enormous bill—in the billions—that we are building up in *unfunded* pension liability (what we'll owe them in the future). If Congress is truly looking for ways to cut the budget, as they claim, they should start with their own retirement plan.

The "Franking" Racket

Another congressional racket is the use of franking privilege. These free mailing privileges are provided to members of Congress, who regularly abuse them at enormous cost to taxpayers. The purpose of the frank is to allow members to mail letters without figuring, or worrying, about postage. For this they each receive an annual postal budget of $108,000.

Sounds good. BUT, members spend most of their franking money in mailing propaganda newsletters to all their constituents on a regular basis in order to advance their reelection, something challengers can't do. This has been going for some time, and, with printing, it costs us an estimated $65 million a year in the House alone.

Only recently have halfhearted restraints been put on the practice. Previously, newsletter-propaganda mass mailings were sent out in an avalanche just before election day. New House rules prohibit mass mailings sixty days prior to election, or about the middle of September.

But clever (devious) congressmen spend just as much money as ever. First, many dump 250,000 pieces of political junk mail in the week preceding the September cutoff. Second, mailings under 500 pieces are excluded from the prohibition, so 499 pieces go out in a continuous stream right up to election day.

John Berthoud, then at the National Taxpayers Union, studied the mailing habits of the congressional species in the 1994 election and found that fifteen dumped large amounts of junk mail right before the deadline. He also found that twenty-seven House members did multiple mailings of 499 or less regularly from the deadline to election day. One congressman from North Carolina mailed batches out *forty-five* times in the two-month period before election day.

What can we do to stop this taxpayer-paid electioneering by incumbents?

Simple. *The House should follow the Senate's lead and declare an election-year ban on all mass mailings.* The savings will be in the millions.

Taxpayer-Paid Vacations

Another, rather presumptuous, racket run by members of both Houses is the "junket." This freebie trip is an affront to citizens, who pay for these expensive vacations by congressmen, their staffs and their wives to the far corners of the globe under the guise of "fact-finding" missions.

The costs are awesome. One magnificent journey was made by four congressmen, their senior staffs and *twenty-five* spouses to China, Japan and Thailand to study the "infrastructure" of those nations. The "fact-finding" became so sophisticated that they spent an entire day at the "Panda Preserve" in China.

The cost? Some $550,000.

Can that be topped? Other junkets come close in jarring the sensibilities of the American public, who, incidentally, have less vacation time than any nation in the Western world, and considerably less than their well-paid elected politicians.

- Twenty-one congressmen, their spouses, staff and guests—a total of more than a hundred persons—

visited the Paris Air Show courtesy of Uncle Sam. Cost? Over $200,000.

- Nineteen House members toured Israel and Saudi Arabia at a cost, to taxpayers, of $322,402. (Who gets the lucrative travel agency business?)
- A House committee member took an "investigative" tour of Eastern Europe with several House members and their spouses: $99,000.
- One ranking senator took a delegation of six and their spouses on a twelve-day trip to the Far East, including Singapore, to investigate "foreign policy." Tab? $359,000.

New Moral Attitude

The MESS in America is paralleled in the halls of Congress, and requires a total revamping of the moral attitude of its members. We will be looking at how to clean up the entire political system, but changes that apply mainly to members of Congress should be separated out in the hope of rebuilding integrity in the declining ethical environment.

Here, then, is the Gross program for reforming unethical congressional behavior.

1. Make sure that legislative and fund-raising activities of members are not mixed—use separate staffs and keep the fund-raising outside the halls of Congress.
2. Require members to regularly disclose their activities on behalf of major contributors, stopping scandals before they start.
3. Members should be prohibited from meeting

personally with regulatory agencies on behalf of their contributors.

4. Eliminate *all perks* now granted members and their staffs.
5. Require members to place their financial holdings in a blind trust. This will eliminate suspicion that they're using inside information or passing legislation that will personally benefit them. It will be considered unethical to the executor of that trust.
6. Pass term-limit legislation (six years for House members; twelve years for senators) to make professional politicians a thing of the past.
7. Close all retirement plans for members except for 401-K plans similar to those in private industry. Present members should not be able to draw down their pensions until they reach the retirement age of sixty-two, regardless of when they leave Congress.
8. Stop most free franking privileges of members of the House and Senate.
9. Institute a strong OMBUDSMAN organization as the watchdog of Congress.
10. Mete out much tougher penalties for unethical behavior.
11. Make public disclosure of all junkets, along with the roster and cost *before* the trip is made.

All these measures are valuable in cleaning up Congress, but eventually it will be necessary to remove money from the political equation, a subject I will turn to shortly.

Meanwhile, the onerous, persuasive, corrosive influence of lobbyists on our susceptible and often greedy politicians has to be squarely faced, which is the subject of our next chapter.

Join me in dissecting still another challenge to American democracy.

7

LOBBYISTS AND CONSULTANTS

The Fourth Branch of Government

Representative Bud Shuster (R., Pa.) is one of the friendliest guys in Congress.

As chairman of the House Transportation and Infrastructure Committee, he rides herd on billions of dollars for roads ($151 billion for the Intermodal Surface Transportation Efficiency Act alone) and shapes the regulations that control much of the transportation business.

Bud loves to share his billions. He is one of Congress's most generous Princes of Pork, rivaling Senator Byrd of West Virginia for the title. His freebie largesse is so legendary that a highway has been named for him in his home district, a slice of small-town Americana which receives an outsize amount of "highway demonstration projects." (Shuster's famous for trying to squeeze a multi-million-dollar monorail into small downtown Altoona!)

Shuster is friendly not only with constituents. He is also close to those who manipulate him and other legislators—the lobbyists, the master influence peddlers of our time. Daily, they seduce the U.S. Congress and the White House to extract that last dollar of taxpayer money for their clients.

The lobbyist he's friendliest with is Ann Eppard. Although somewhat new to the lobbying game, she's a veteran of government service who has learned that you can earn ten times as much by cashing in. Eppard was Shuster's chief of staff, and as he says: "She's been my right arm for over twenty-five years."

Ms. Eppard is still quite important to the congressman. After taking early retirement in 1994, she set herself up as a successful lobbyist, capitalizing on her easy access to Congress, and especially to Mr. Shuster.

Her clients? Naturally, people who wanted to reach Shuster's committee, including Conrail, Federal Express, Union Pacific, United Airlines and Sea-Land. Even Amtrak, a government-subsidized operation, awarded her a $100,000 contract, a form of political incest in which Ms. Eppard was back drinking at the government trough.

Permissive Rules

Government regulations prohibit former senior staffers like Ms. Eppard from lobbying their former bosses for a year. BUT in a sidestepping of morality typical of government rules, she could and did lobby his committee, including the staff chief. Since November 1995, the one-year exclusion has been over and she can directly lobby her former boss, and does, with gusto.

How about friendship? Now that she's no longer Shuster's aide-de-camp, are there ties that go beyond the simple politico-lobbyist relationship?

You bet your sweet, often worthless, vote. Ms. Eppard became Shuster's leading fund-raiser and political consultant for his district, for which he paid her another $36,000—on top of her federal pension and lobbyist income. No slouch she, Eppard helped raise $655,000 for Shuster in 1995 alone.

Like Shuster, Eppard is truly friendly. She drives the congressman to and from work—from his home to Capitol Hill—and on several occasions Shuster has stayed over at her town house in Alexandria. In fact, even Mrs. Shuster, who lives in Pennsylvania, has joined her husband at Ms. Eppard's place.

Is she grateful for his launching her as a lobbyist, work which brings in at least $600,000 a year, considerably more than her government salary of $108,000? Judge for yourself. Ms. Eppard organized a fund-raiser in which her transportation clients immortalized Bud by paying for a portrait of the chairman. It is now displayed in the committee's hearing room.

The politically incestuous relationship between lawmaker and lobbyist can stimulate feelings of nausea among the public. But Mr. Shuster is unmoved. "This goes on all the time around this town," Shuster told a reporter for the *Journal of Commerce*. The difference, he said, is that he's open about the connection.

In March 1996, Common Cause filed a complaint

against Shuster, asking the House Ethics Committee to investigate whether Shuster is, in fact, violating rules governing members' conduct.

"Either the Ethics Committee must find that Representative Shuster's activities violate the House ethics rules," said Common Cause, "or the Committee should tell the American people that, in its view, what Representative Shuster has done is acceptable and ethical behavior."

Whatever the unpredictable Ethics Committee decides (a wrist slap, a wink, or a reprimand), the whole thing has the aroma of a barnyard. We can hardly rely on the Committee or the permissive rules of the Congress to break up lobbyist-politician money-for-favor deals. If we're ever to have clean government—which we surely don't have now—a new set of lobbying rules has to be promulgated, something which I will attempt at the end of this chapter.

Mutual Affection

Politicians and lobbyists are involved in one of the great romances of the last quarter of the twentieth century. It is based on mutual need, which then builds mutual affection.

For lobbyists, the politicians are the open sesame that justifies their enormous fees. Even the smallest of clauses within the recent Telecommunications Reform Act of 1995, or the annual revision in the IRS code, contain legislative wonders that can save, or give, corporations and industries, and even powerful individuals, multimillion dollars.

The cash involved is hundreds of times greater than the salaries of lobbyists who crowd "Gucci Gulch," the hallways outside 1100 Longworth, the hearing room of the House Ways and Means Committee, or the open spaces outside 215 Dirksen Office Building, the home of the Senate Finance Committee. Packed like gourmet anchovies, the lobbyists wait breathlessly during tax bill "mark up" days for news of whether their exemptions or changes have been passed.

(The origin of "Gucci Gulch" seems to have been the fashion for many years, of lobbyists wearing expensive, tasseled Gucci loafers.)

For politicians, lobbyist/influence peddlers are welcome in an inner club that provides help in the drafting of bills and the "education" of legislators too lazy to do intense research. The pièce de résistance of the lobbyist calling is of course large contributions for the politician's campaigns—the lifeblood of the corrupt system we lovingly refer to as American democracy.

The money comes from $10,000 PAC contributions, a number of $1,000 "hard money" contributions from themselves and other individuals in their lawyer, lobbying or client firms, plus *molto grande* six-figure "soft money" contributions from their corporate clients.

No wonder lobbyists, now joined by the newly powerful ranks of the political consultants, have come to be known as the *Fourth Branch of Government*—right after the original three of the legislative, judicial and executive.

Part of their power rests on that expensive intangible: friendship. Friendship between lobbyists and their marks? Absolutely. As Mr. Shuster points out, it goes on all the time, apparently a logical result of peddlers and legislators working alongside each other, both taking time out to scratch each other's back.

Clever lobbyists become personally attached to the most important of their politicians, making it much easier to obtain the favors that sustain their profession.

Lobbyists as Friends

Take the presidency. Mr. Clinton's closest pal is probably James Blair, chief counsel and informal lobbyist for Tyson Foods. That friendship provided $100,000 to Hillary Clinton in a cattle futures trading deal that was actually a gift to HRC. There were also numerous favors for the chicken company both in Arkansas and more recently in Washington. Their reciprocal arrangement is satisfying to both. The Clintons often stay at the Blair home in Arkansas, and the Blairs stayed over at the White House on inauguration night, reportedly in the Lincoln Room.

Betsey Wright, who was Clinton's chief of staff as governor of Arkansas, is now part of the powerful Wexler Group lobbyists, and easily brings her clients to the attention of the chief executive, his staff and his cabinet.

Ms. Wright's many clients include the American Dietetic Association (ADA), which represents 64,000 dieticians and nutritional specialists. She lobbied Mrs. Clinton to be sure their services would be covered under the First Lady's proposed national health system. Mrs. Clinton helped set up three meetings between the ADA and top government officials, and the dieticians were included in her since-aborted plan. Having perfect access to the President himself, Wright even pitched one of her clients to him while he was watching a University of Arkansas basketball game!

Reagan's administration was no less efficient in populating the lobby world. Among former White House officials who became lobbyists were Michael Deaver, image maker for Reagan, and Oval Office strategist Lynn Nofziger, both of whom got into trouble for breaking lobbying rules.

In the case of the Congress, daily contact with lobbyists binds them as well. In his now-famous diary, Republican Senator Robert Packwood explained his close relationship with his lobbyist pal Ronald Crawford, and how it cost taxpayers millions. Crawford was a successful lobbyist for several large groups including the American Iron and Steel Institute, Pharmaceutical Manufacturers' Association, Shell Oil, Northrop, even General Motors.

Crawford's wife was employed in Packwood's office and the senator helped her become a commissioner on the International Trade Commission during the Bush administration.

The friendly lobbyist couldn't do enough for Packwood, nor Packwood for him. Crawford raised money for Packwood's campaigns and threw a party each year for the senator's staff, paid for by a client. The Crawfords and the Packwoods were pals, the kind of relationship that pays off for expert lobbyists.

Attracted to Power

Crawford probably found Packwood charming, but it's more certain that he was attracted to Packwood's power as the ranking member of the Senate Finance Committee, through which all money bills flow.

(The friendship between them, Mrs. Packwood told the Senate Ethics Committee, was "both social and political." But in Washington, she added, "it's pretty murky" which is which.)

Packwood was an easy mark, as are a number of politicians. In one incident, when Crawford had a tax problem with a client involving the transfer of assets among company partners, he turned to his friend Bob Packwood.

Could the senator help out? He sure could, confirming that *quid pro quo*, the slogan of Beltway lobbyists, is rapidly replacing *E Pluribus Unum* as the national rallying call.

"His client was Shell Oil, and this was very, very important to him personally," Packwood relates—or confesses—in his diary. "He said: 'I know how much you hate the oil companies.' I said: 'Ron, I still hate the oil companies, but I'll do you a favor.' "

With Packwood's help, the Committee approved a bill that saved Shell taxes.

When Packwood feared the cost of alimony for his divorced wife, he sought a job for her from his friendly lobbyists, most of whom quickly agreed to help. One lobbyist offered her $37,500 for five years of part-time work, then added the key: "If you become head of the Senate

Finance Committee," he told Packwood, "I can probably double that."

Politicians are often in awe of the financial success of lobbyists, who earn anywhere from $200,000 to $1 million. Packwood expressed it best when he told his diary that perhaps someday, "I can become a lobbyist at five or six hundred thousand" dollars a year.

Like a lot of politicians, Packwood enjoyed the rich ambience of the lobbyist's world. He wrote of attending a $1,269 dinner for ten, toasting from $70 bottles of wine. At the dinner, he received an offer of $3,000 from a paper company, which he initially scoffed at because of the wealth of the donors. Then he thought better of it, writing like a reconciled panhandler: "I'm glad to get anything I can get."

Many-Splendored Thing

The politician-lobbyist relationship has many sides to it. Lobbyists are the gatekeepers for many PACs, which bring in more than half of all congressional war chests. A single lobbyist might handle fifteen clients, and be able to hand out up to $150,000 to any favored congressman. Getting that money requires a kind of dance by politicians, especially the increasingly popular funfest, replete with food.

They're called PAC parties, and pols charge about $500 a head for each lobbyist-PACman who attends, a kind of mass influence-peddling ritual. In 1994, Representative Richard Lehman of California threw one featuring asparagus and other farm victuals grown in his home district. Representative John Boehner of Ohio gave a popular annual "Beach Party" for lobbyists, replete with palm trees, beach music and optional surf dress—all held in the American Legion Hall just blocks from the Capitol.

So regularly are these events thrown for lobbyists, that professional party givers are working for congressmen, getting about $2,500 per party for arranging everything including invitations. (Now, we're talking real democracy!)

How big a business is Washington lobbying and how many players are there?

Lobbying is Washington's second-largest industry, after government. No one really knows the cash flow of all lobbyists, but just the PAC spending they control runs several hundred million dollars a year. Estimates on the total size of the industry go up over a billion dollars a year.

There are now 9,219 individuals registered with the Secretary of the Senate, somewhat of an increase because of the new Lobbying Disclosure Act of 1995, which hopes to snare unregistered influence peddlers. The old law only covered those who lobbied Congress, while the new law includes those trying to influence the executive branch as well.

Who Is a Lobbyist?

How is someone defined as a lobbyist? The new law requires that anyone who meets the following criteria must register with both the Senate and the House, even if they are lobbying the White House as well. The penalty for nonregistration is a $50,000 fine.

1. Anyone who spends 20 percent of their time trying to influence government.
2. Those who receive compensation of at least $5,000 as a lobbyist in a six month period.
3. Organizations that spend $20,000 on lobbying in any six-month period.

The registration is for law firms, lobbying firms, public relations companies, self-employed lobbyists, trade associations, public policy groups and corporations which have in-house lobbying operations.

Each of the lobbying firms must register itself and list its employees who are working as lobbyists as well. Twice a year it also has to declare its lobbying income by client, and its area of interest. The eventual registration will be well over 10,000, to which we have to add the army of supporting clerical and executive talent. This probably raises the size of the Washington lobby industry to 25,000.

Clients of lobbying firms who don't have in-house people need not register, but they're an integral part of the business. Their names turn up when listed by the lobbying firms. Patton, Boggs & Blow, for instance, perhaps Washington's largest law/lobby firm, has registered 124 clients with the U.S. Senate. There are thousands of such firms listed, but they manage to escape registration because they don't specifically have an "in-house lobbyist." (Probably a failing in the law.)

NEITHER do the numbers reflect the fastest-growing part of the lobbying business—the statehouse and city lobbyists, who generally have to register locally and, as we shall see, are rivaling their Washington cousins.

Because of the stronger disclosure and registration requirements, the new federal lobbying law sounds good. But in reality it's almost useless, and absolutely no roadblock against more lobbying. As long as lobbyists can provide politicians with money for their campaigns, what difference does it make who's registered and who's not?

It makes not a whit of difference, especially since under the new law lobbyists don't have to declare the name of the politician who's the object of their affections.

In any case, the new law *does not restrain lobbyists*, it merely announces them—somewhat.

Singular Gain

There has been one small improvement in the lobbying racket. Prior to 1996, members of Congress could go on lobbyist-sponsored golf, tennis and other leisure trips, with their spouses, all expenses paid and all "ethical." They could also receive up to $250 in cash or other gifts from each lobbyist, with luncheons and dinners of $100 or less not counting toward the $250 maximum. It was an invitation to legal bribery, which went on routinely.

Now, as a result of public pressure and disclosure (including my book, *A Call for Revolution: How Washington Is Strangling America* and other of my works), politicians have been moved to action. Last summer, prompted by Senator Paul Wellstone of Minnesota—who happens to be the No. 1 spender and No. 1 reformer in the Senate, an exasperating combination—the Senate changed its gift rules. Henceforth, all gifts over $50, and up to $100 from a single source, were prohibited, as were free trips paid for by lobbyists, even for charity causes, which was a favored gimmick.

The House, led by Representative Chris Shays of Connecticut and Linda Smith of Washington State, went even further. Their new rules cutting out virtually all gifts went into effect on January 1, 1996.

They cut down the most obvious bribes, other than the giant PAC contributions controlled by lobbyists, the true source of corruption. The new law prohibits free meals and travel supplied by lobbyists. It definitely cleans up a little of the foul air in Washington, but it has loopholes large enough to pass an elephant (or a donkey) through.

As a *New York Times* editorial commented: "Just how the members of the House interpret these rules will have to be carefully monitored to make sure they do not become escape hatches for the kind of corrupt practices that have brought discredit to Congress in the past."

Gift Manual

To explain what congressmen and their staffs can and cannot do under present rules (other than accept a small fortune from lobbyists for their campaigns), the House Ethics Committee has issued a ten-page pony.

It bans gifts except for those from "personal friends," relatives and other members and staff of Congress. The new rule guide has twenty-three examples, including the following:

"A rotary club in Maxwell Member's district holds

periodic luncheon meetings of its membership and invites him to one. Maxwell may attend and eat lunch."

BUT "Owner Owen, the owner of a sports team, invites Maury Member to view an upcoming game from his skybox. . . . If Maury wishes to attend the game, he must buy his own ticket."

Does this take generous lobbyists out of the gift loop?

Not exactly.

"Joe College was Roy Representative's college roommate," says the coda. "Every year since they were freshmen, Joe has sent Roy a sweater on his birthday. Two years ago, Joe became a lobbyist for the Widget Association. He has continued to send sweaters on Roy's birthday. . . . On his birthday in 1996 (despite the new rules), Roy may accept the sweater."

(Should we assume that lobbying firms are now avidly looking to hire "personal friends" of politicians such as those close to former senator Packwood, who, incidentally, is launching his own Washington lobby operation?)

The new lobbying law doesn't seem to frighten lobbyist leaders, who are already planning how to exploit loopholes. Thomas M. Susman, chairman of the American League of Lobbyists' panel on ethics, predicts a shift of funds from outright gifts to larger campaign contributions to the same politician. Wright Andrews, president of the League, smiles at the mention of congressional reforms, secure in his knowledge of the Golden Rule—he who has the gold, rules. Speaking of the loopholes, Andrews says: "I would prefer to call them pathways, or, in some cases, interstates."

There are several gimmicks available to outwit reformers. One idea is for the congressman to reverse the roles and hold a one-man fund-raiser at an expensive restaurant. *He* entertains the lobbyist. The member picks up the $200 lunch tab from his campaign fund, but walks away with a $5,000 contribution!

"It's ludicrous to think a free dinner will buy off a member but that a $5,000 check won't," notes Ronald Shaiko, a government professor at American University in Washington, quoted in *Business Week.*

Afterlife of a Congressman

There's one needed lobbying reform that Congress avoids like the proverbial ten-foot pole. That's a big perk that affects only them, and satisfies the dreams of people like Packwood.

In involves the afterlife of politicians. **What happens when members of the House and Senate are defeated or retire?** Do they just fade away?

No way. They so love Washington and the glamour and financial rewards of its life that the majority of ex-congressmen do not head home to Kalamazoo, as they should. They stay in the humid but celebrity-driven ambience of Washington. And do what?

What do you think? *Of the last ninety-one ex-congressmen who stayed in Washington after their term, eighty-one became lobbyists*, generally earning two to three times their government salary from the influence-peddling get-go. They proceed to carry out Bob Packwood's dream, proceeding toward the seven-figure heaven.

It's obvious that a former congressman (or -woman) who has spent years building relationships with colleagues is going to be valuable once he leaves. For one year, he is not permitted to lobby Congress, but after that, there are no holds barred. The result is that the city is filled with hundreds of rich former congressmen, now trading on their friendships and expertise.

The foolish part of the one-year restriction is that it applies only to lobbying the House and Senate. From day one, the "Former" can lobby the executive branch, enabling lobbying firms to *immediately* hire the new stars of the influence-selling business.

There's also a little-known perk granted former congressmen that is denied to other lobbyists. Lobbyists can gather *outside* the congressional chambers but they're stopped at the door of the House and Senate as members enter. But not former congressman-lobbyists. Each Former has a special pass issued by Congress that gets him into the cloakrooms, where he can have coffee and drinks with his colleagues.

When the bell rings for a congressional vote, the Former just puts his arm around his mark, flashes his million-dollar pass to the doorkeeper and walks right onto the floor of his onetime home—Nirvana for a lobbyist. Talk about influence-peddling; this is influence-marketing.

How long does he hold this floor privilege? A year or two after he has gone from Capitol Hill? Don't be naive. *He is allowed to cash in for life!*

Tales of the Formers

Some Formers are truly blessed with chutzpah. Representative George Miller (D., California) was surprised when he walked into the hearing room of a House resource subcommittee dealing with water and power. On the dais with the congressmen was a lobbyist—ex-congressman John Rhodes III (R., Arizona), who had once been on the committee and was now cashing in as a member of a law/lobby firm. In fact, he was getting $96,000 a year from water users in Arizona. Only when Miller complained did the chairman ask the lobbyist to get down off his high dais.

Another Former, Democrat Toby Moffett of Connecticut, started off as an eager public policy advocate for Ralph Nader—a so-called Nader Raider. Then he became a congressman, serving three terms. A popular politician who made friends easily, he ran unsuccessfully for senator and governor, only to eventually return to Washington and the lobby business.

Starting with the Wexler lobbying group, Moffett found it easy to ply the phone, making contacts with old friends on the Hill, Republicans and Democrats alike. "At Wexler, I'd make a phone call to a particular member, directly, maybe at home let's say, on a critical thing and get some feedback or information that's worth millions of dollars to somebody," he's quoted in *Washington Monthly*.

Moffett then left Wexler for greener pastures with a large law/lobbying firm where he had such clients as Coopers and Lybrand, one of the large accounting firms. It was a long way from his Nader days. When several of his old friends lost their seats in Congress, Moffett had them all over for dinner, reassuring them that there was life—a very good life—after Congress.

The revolving door of the lobbying world brings former government officials, from Congress and the executive branch, into it, in droves. Many lobbyists are quite prominent people, often in the news, with recognizable names and impressive backgrounds.

Mike Deaver, who was President Reagan's brilliant media adviser, ended up first on the cover of *Time*, then as a lobbyist for many firms anxious to get the ear of the White House. He was then convicted of perjury, and performed community service, only to return to the lobbying world, where he's doing quite well, thank you, especially since the Republicans have taken Congress.

On the other side of the political spectrum, Susan Thomases, Hillary Clinton's personal lawyer, has used her White House reputation to influence both clients and government officials. Representing a group of Puerto Rican companies in a dispute with HUD, she reportedly got the attorney representing the Puerto Ricans an interview with the chief of staff at HUD. Her other clients, suitably impressed by her closeness to the First Lady, even include Morgan and Company, a symbol of economic royalism once despised by good Democrats.

The lobbyist ranks also include Robin Dole, the Majority Leader's daughter, who worked for Century 21 real estate; and former congressman Vin Weber, a leader in Jack Kemp's Empower America movement.

There can be party backscratching, but party lines can also be waived in the lobbying world, where the big buck outweighs ideologies. Former Democratic Congressman Tom Downey of New York, a firebrand liberal on the House Ways and Means Committee, has joined with former Republican Congressman Rod Chandler of Washington State, also once of Ways and Means, as a lobbyist.

What separated them has all been healed by cash.

The Executive Branch

The executive branch people also have their gilded afterlife. Frank Donatelli, former political director of the Reagan White House, crossed party lines as well to work with Texas Democrat Bob Strauss at Akin, Gump.

The whole question of lobbying by former executive branch officials, including White House staff, became the subject of a presidential edict. When Mr. Clinton took office, he passionately decried the power of "influence peddlers," as he called lobbyists, and vowed to clean up Washington.

When his transition team hired some three thousand political appointees, from cabinet officers to deputy assistant secretaries, the President warned them. They had better not try to lobby the people they had helped hire. He wouldn't tolerate it.

Was that true? Of course not.

How long a lobbying ban was he putting in? Five years? Three years? Guess again. After *six months* they could lobby away at the very people they had hired!

The President went even further in his reform promises, proudly announcing that there would no longer be a revolving door of government service to lobbyist ranks.

Was that true? Of course not.

Let's examine his Executive Order #112834, issued January 20, 1993, which impressed the media and the naive. Before that, federal statutes were quitc loosc about lobbying. In fact, they were farcical.

Cabinet officers, after they left government, could become lobbyists after waiting only one year. Other senior personnel had a similar minor restriction.

The President now supposedly tightened the rules. Henceforth, the White House announced, senior officials would have to wait *five years* before joining the happy lobbyists on K Street.

Again, was it true? No way.

The restriction applied only to the agency where they had worked! Except for members of the cabinet, who really had to wait a year, the others—White House and cabinet staffers—could become high-priced influence peddlers the very next day after leaving the executive branch!

It's done by a simple evasive process. Instead of lobbying the Department of Agriculture, where they had worked, for example, they merely turned their love to their buddies in Commerce or Energy.

Besides, there was another whole world open to them. There is no restriction whatsoever on former government executives lobbying the people they dealt with in Congress. Not even a day's delay.

Trading Away America

The greatest farce, with comic overtones, involved the trade representatives. The Office of the U.S. Trade Representative is headed by a member of the president's cabinet. He, or she, and the staff do the trade negotiating with foreign countries, deals that have proven very detrimental to America, which now carries an enormous trade deficit of some $150 billion. Many economists believe that is translated as a loss of some six million jobs—one job shopped overseas for every $25,000 in deficit.

Selling out in this area was, and is, quite routine and easy. A study done by the Center for Public Integrity reveals the worst. Our trade people have routinely been playing both sides of the field, working first for Uncle Sam, then for Japan or Germany or France, then back again for our government.

The shocking truth is that from 1974 to 1990, almost half (47 percent) of all senior U.S. representatives or their firms have registered with the Justice Department as "Foreign Agents" after they left office. Based on a 1930s law that forced Americans working for Nazi Germany to register, it has since been expanded to include Americans lobbying for any nation.

The firm of William Eberle, a former head of the agency, lobbied for Nissan. Harald Malmgren, former deputy trade representative, worked for the Japan Whaling Association and the Japan External Trade Organization. Steven Saunders worked as assistant U.S. trade representative for a year and a half. Within nine months, Saunders and Company was on retainer to the Japanese embassy.

William Walker, former deputy trade representative, has worked for Toshiba and the Japanese semiconductor industry, which for years tried to put our chipmakers out of business. Doral Cooper, former assistant U.S. trade rep, was responsible for the Pacific Basin. Two weeks after quitting the government, she was in South Korea working for Mike Deaver's lobbying firm.

William Brock, former top trade representative, formed the Brock Group in 1989. His firm has since worked for Toyota, Taiwan and Airbus, the competitor to American plane builders.

It's not only that our trade people desert the nation after they serve, but they often come into the office already tainted as Foreign Agents.

Carla Hills, who had been our top trade person, had represented several Asian firms including Daewoo Electronics, Matsushita and Panasonic before being named to the cabinet.

Her deputy, S. Linn Williams, had worked in Tokyo as an attorney for Nissan, Nomura Securities and Orient Finance. Another top deputy, trade rep Julius Katz, headed a company that did analyses for twenty-eight foreign clients including Japan Trade Center, Toyota and Cartier International.

The Office of the U.S. Trade Representative apparently has little concern for conflict-of-interest. At the same time Katz was working for foreign clients, for instance, he was also a paid consultant for our Trade office!

Bipartisan Damage

The people listed above all served in Republican administrations, but working for foreign governments is a bipartisan affliction. The current trade representative, Democrat Mickey Kantor, who was also Clinton's campaign chairman, was a partner in a law firm that had represented the Japanese electronics giant NEC.

President Clinton, while running for president, had eight presidential advisers who personally, or whose firms, had worked for foreign governments or companies. Several were even registered as Foreign Agents. They included Thomas Hoog, a vice chairman of Hill and Knowlton, who handled the embassy of the People's Republic of China.

Clinton adviser Paula Stern, who had chaired the International Trade Commission, had testified before her old agency for the Japanese Display Industry. Clintonite attorney Samuel Berger, a former Carter administration official, was also a registered Foreign Agent. His firm represented no one less than the embassy of Japan.

Other prominent Foreign Agents, who now number seven hundred registered with the Department of Justice, have included William Colby, former CIA director; Frank Mankiewicz, chief aide to the late senator Robert Kennedy; Richard Allen, national security adviser to President Reagan; Paul Warnke, strategic arms negotiator for President Carter.

And people wonder why we have such a high trade deficit.

BUT President Clinton vowed that he would clean all that up. Has he? Of course not.

In his inaugural executive order, he *ostensibly* put a reform edict about trade representatives into effect. In Executive Order #112834, the President addressed the problem with the following new rule: HENCEFORTH ANYONE INVOLVED IN A TRADE NEGOTIATION

WOULD HAVE TO PLEDGE THAT HE WOULD NOT WORK FOR OR LOBBY FOR A FOREIGN GOVERNMENT OR BUSINESS FOR FIVE YEARS FOLLOWING HIS WORK IN THE U.S. TRADE REPRESENTATIVE'S OFFICE.

Sound good? Surely. The press hailed the reform and gave it high kudos. The only problem was that it, too, was a fake.

"That rule on trade negotiators waiting five years before becoming lobbyists in postgovernment employment has never been put into effect," says a spokesman for the Office of Government Ethics. "To be operational, the people involved would have to take a pledge that they were involved in a trade negotiation, and therefore bound by the presidential rule. To date [over three years later], no one has signed such a pledge."

Dual Role

Among the most powerful—and dangerous—of all lobbyists are the chairmen of our two political parties, who move effortlessly from their quasi-public work in and out of government and law practice and lobbying work, building an enormous income for themselves in the process.

There are no conflict-of-interest laws governing these political bosses because they are private citizens working for private parties and are not on the federal payroll. BUT they wield enormous power, both as politicians and as lobbyists.

As we have seen, there is only a thin line between private political parties and public operations.

Party chairmen often meet with presidents (when their party controls the Oval Office) and attend such closed-door meetings in Congress as the Deputy Whip's strategy meetings on Wednesday morning where legislative work and votes are discussed.

Are they outsiders or public servants?

That's the dilemma for democracy when it comes to political parties and their bosses. We can't decide if they are fish or fowl. (No pun intended.) They are privy to and can influence government policy and federal appointees enormously, yet they earn their money—much of the time—from sources other than the party.

Many of the party chairmen are on both the party and other payrolls at the same time. Half of all the party chairmen in both parties had a separate income, often from law/lobby firms. *And most startling, unless they died or left Washington, all of them became lobbyists after leaving office.* In addition, the Center for Public Integrity found that since 1977, half of all party chairmen were registered with the Justice Department as Foreign Agents, receiving income from foreign nations or corporations.

The ethical lines of chairmen of the two major parties are so blurred that people closely involved seem to have lost perspective on what is right and wrong. Timothy May, managing partner of Patton, Boggs, in discussing possible conflict-of-interest for party chairmen still working as lobbyists, commented that it was ridiculous for them not to "employ their influence to help their clients." He added that there's only a conflict if helping clients "would damage the interests of the party."

The lobbying kingdom in Washington continues to

rule supreme because it also controls many of the purse strings that politicians need to run their campaigns—an interlocking conspiracy that is destroying our democracy.

State Lobbyists

But Washington is not the only site of "legal corruption." Increasingly, local lobbying networks are gaining power with our elected state officials. Unfortunately, states are even more lax than the federal government in controlling the situation. In the shadow of attention given to Washington, local lobbyists are getting away with political murder.

The roster of nonfederal lobbyists is much longer than the Washington one, by a factor of some four to one. One study estimated state lobbyist ranks at 42,000, not counting city and county lobbyists. Just the small state of Connecticut has 2,700 lobbyists, one fourth the Washington total.

In California, where state legislators are well paid ($75,600), there is no limit on outside income, so lawyer/lobbyists serving in the legislature have a clear field. Not only can they continue their law practice while in office, drawing a full salary, but they can also be lobbyists at the same time!

Naturally, they can't lobby the state, but they can lobby counties, towns, even large cities like Los Angeles or San Francisco for their clients, even though they are elected officials. The same is true in many states. *Incroyable.*

Is California less strict than other states? Absolutely not. The same laxity—or better still, hanky-panky—holds true nationwide, and will only get worse. The return of many functions from Washington to the states, while desperately needed, will increase the amount of money being funneled into states, and thus increase the ranks and power of local lobbyists, many of whom control PACs.

In California, corporations and labor unions do not need a PAC. Unlike under the federal law, they can contribute directly to candidates, guided by the sure hand of lobbyists who know the political landscape. Philip Morris gave a $125,000 contribution to one challenger for the state legislature, who effectively used it to defeat the incumbent.

(The whole question of political ethics at a state level is still a fifty-part crazy quilt. Most states have some sort of conflict-of-interest law, for example, but that doesn't stop some clever politicians from cashing in. In Arkansas, for example, we saw Governor Bill Clinton going into partnership with the head of a bank that he was regulating. In Tennessee, Governor Lamar Alexander, who ran for the Republican presidential nomination, was able to invest $20,000 in three business deals while in office, and come out $1.9 million richer.)

The states have a very uneven record of controlling lobbyists and their seduction of lawmakers. According to the Council on Governmental Ethics Laws (COGEL), only twenty-seven states have any kind of a ban on gifts from lobbyists. Only one—Wisconsin—has an outright ban of all gifts, including meals. New Jersey has a similar total ban, but it only applies to the executive branch. (State legislators like freebies!)

Florida has a $100 gift limit, but no limit on the aggregate amount lawmakers can take. The same is true of Idaho, where legislators can take $50 at a time, as many times as they want. California permits each legislator to collect $280 in gifts and free meals *per* lobbyist. The state legislator with fifty lobbyist friends can eat pretty well on the house.

Most of the other twenty-seven states that have some kind of ban do permit free meals and beverages from lobbyists, and several allow "entertainment." That's the case with Arizona, which also permits "travel."

Lax Enforcement

Some states are very lax in enforcing their lobbying laws, but occasionally some do clamp down, even if it requires federal intervention. In 1994, the U.S. Attorney's Office indicted Maryland's leading lobbyist, Bruce C. Bereano, not for giving gifts but for covering up illegal campaign contributions to members.

Bereano allegedly encouraged employees to make campaign donations, then reimbursed them himself. He also gave money to relatives so they could donate to his favored legislators. To recoup the money, he allegedly overcharged his lobby clients $16,000 for "entertainment."

Bereano, according to the U.S. Attorney's Office in Baltimore, was convicted on seven counts of mail fraud but received only six months probation and was not sentenced to jail. He is back lobbying the state legislature as before.

The entire process of paid lobbying is increasingly creating a distortion of democracy. The lobby industry likes to quote the First Amendment of the Constitution, which gives the people the right "to petition the government for a redress of grievances."

True, but there's a distinct difference between citizen's rights and lobbying as it now operates. Most Americans can only petition Congress in their spare moments, and at a minimum of cost by writing, phoning or faxing their congressmen. (Missives to the White House are a waste of time.)

Registered lobbyists, on the other hand, have hundreds of thousands of dollars—perhaps millions—to spend hounding members of Congress, physically tailing them, working the offices, halls and committee rooms eight hours a day, then contributing heavily to members' campaigns. They even seem to be part of the legislative process, gaining the access that's unavailable to regular citizens.

Intolerable Situation

There's no doubt that the present operation of lobbying in America is intolerable to a free people.

Can we do anything about it?

Quite a lot. I have developed a nine-point plan, which, if adopted, will go a long way toward cleaning this aspect of soiled democracy.

As follows:

1. Members of the House and Senate shall be prohibited from lobbying Congress, the executive or any branch of government, for five years after they leave office, encouraging them to return home where they came from, and now belong.

2. No member of the executive branch shall lobby any member of the government, including Congress, for a period of five years after leaving government employ.
3. No staff member of a congressman, or someone who works for a congressional committee, shall be allowed to lobby either Congress or any branch of government for five years after leaving that job.
4. No registered lobbyist may be in charge of, or connected in any way with, a Political Action Committee (PAC).
5. Just as members of the House can no longer accept free meals or entertainment, so no member of either house of Congress shall be permitted to offer meals, refreshments or entertainment to any registered lobbyist. PAC parties given by members to raise money shall no longer be allowed.
6. Lobbyists' semi-annual reports to Congress shall henceforth include the name of the member, committee or staffer lobbied and the amount spent.
7. The present right of former congressmen to enter the floor of either House and to use the cloakrooms shall be revoked. No former members of Congress shall have any rights at congressional hearings that are not granted to other citizens.
8. No member of the executive branch at or above the GS-9 level shall ever be permitted to register as a Foreign Agent after leaving government service. The same shall be true of all members of Congress and their senior staff.

9. No member of the U.S. Office of Trade Representative shall ever be permitted to register as a Foreign Agent. No one who has ever registered as Foreign Agent shall be allowed to serve in the U.S. Office of Trade Representative.

The states should follow the same rules. (Other than those affecting Foreign Agents.) That's not easy, since each state has separate regulations. But citizens should pressure state legislatures to clean up gift-giving to members and the revolving door of legislator-turned-lobbyist.

Even though legislation to control party heads is difficult, stronger ethical rules should be put in place to restrain them on both the national and state levels. No former lobbyist should be allowed to serve as head or deputy head of our parties, nor should they later be permitted to cash in and become lobbyists.

In the Democratic and Republican National Committees, strict party rules should also limit the chairman and deputy chairman from having been, or ever becoming, Foreign Agents.

We should ask for nothing less.

The World of Consultants

The other portion of the Fourth Branch of government is the new "profession" (you should excuse the expression) of Paid Political Consultants. They have always been with us, but no aspect of the political world has grown as rapidly in recent years. Twenty years ago, most people working with candidates were volunteers, people of similar mind and ideology, friends, even relatives.

But these "amateurs" are increasingly being pushed out by professionals as the dollars involved escalate and the desire to win assumes the competitive energy of an Olympic contest.

Their ranks include campaign managers, pollsters, mail-order specialists, fund-raisers, public relations people, television and radio advertising specialists, strategists and consultants wearing two hats: 1. advising candidates on how to position themselves and their issues as well as 2. advising public officials on how to tailor their thinking to raise their popularity and poll numbers.

It is a massive industry which swallows up most of the $1.5 billion spent on all political races in the presidential election years. Politics has become mass marketing, and there are swarms of marketing "experts" willing to lend a hand for a fee.

There are some stars in the field: Dick Morris, the late Lee Atwater, Ed Rollins, Bob Squirer, James Carville, Frank Luntz. But for each well-known consultant, there are thousands of "operatives," as they are sometimes called, who move from candidate to candidate and campaign to campaign, selling their services, often at outrageously high prices.

Like lobbying, consulting is a big-money business. A check of Federal Elections Commission documents shows that in one three-month period, for instance, pollster Stanley Greenberg received $365,000 from the DNC, and sizable sums also went to James Carville, Paul Begala and Mandy Grunwald, all of whom have been regulars at the White House.

These and other paid consultants may operate in the

White House as private citizens, but they have the power of high officials, a growing, if frightening, trend of "off the books" government. There is absolutely no check on their activities, no accountability and no ethical rules that need to be obeyed.

"You have an adjunct kind of shadow government," says Charles Lewis of the Center for Public Integrity. "They will do whatever they need to do to help Bill and also to remain robust in the private sector. There is a yuppie arrogance: 'We're the good guys, don't bust our chops.' "

The star consultants sometimes rival the candidates themselves in the attention and publicity focused on them. The media has given James Carville much of the credit for the 1992 Clinton victory, just as the late Lee Atwater—a similar unconventional type—was credited with the Bush victory of 1988. Carville, who is from Louisiana and is often called the "Ragin' Cajun," hardly looks or sounds like the polished Beltway pros, and is fond of spouting off on anything involving politics.

Those Negative Ads

The rise of the ranks and power of consultants in our election system has had a strong, and worrisome, side effect. Along with it has come an increased emphasis on television political ads, their most potent weapon in influencing the public. This has triggered a national debate, especially about what is termed "negative" advertising—attacks on the person or record of opponents.

When the advertising community, specifically the American Association of Advertising Agencies, assailed much of this political advertising as misleading and false, Carville bit back. Speaking before the American Association of Political Consultants (AAPC), who gave him their "Campaign Manager of the Year" award, Carville said that "the people who brought us the Marlboro Man and the Pinto gas tank cover-up ought to crawl back under the rocks that they came from."

(The AAPC that heard Carville is an organization of 750 top consultants in the country, run strictly on a bipartisan basis with eighteen Republicans and eighteen Democrats on the board and with a rotating presidency. One of the newest trends in the political operative world, they explain, is the Internet, which the organization expects will strongly influence the political process in the coming century.)

James Carville may well be right about the sins of American advertising in general, but that hardly excuses negative political advertising in America, which is increasingly becoming the shame of American democracy.

The press has lately taken to exposing evasions, distortions, half-truths and even outright lies in political ads. They are generally correct. In every political career, there are statements and votes that can be twisted to make one's opponents look bad. Even the truth, when gussied up and "spun," can appear to be damaging.

If the "sound bite" is offensive to better democracy, then the "negative" political ad is truly destructive. Yet not only does it live on, it proliferates, gaining currency not just in federal elections but in campaigns down to the state, and even the local, level.

The cost of these ads is enormous, annually pushing

up the cost of campaigns, a phenomenon we saw in the 1996 Republican primaries. They take some 40 percent of all the money now being expended in campaigns. They are destructive to the democratic ethos as well. In a new book, *Going Negative,* two political scientists—one from MIT, the other from UCLA—show that political television advertising actually reduces the voter turnout by creating cynicism about the process.

They estimate that in 1992 it cut the turnout by 6 million votes, hardly an endorsement. The tragedy is that people *do* believe political attack ads and they do work better than positive ones. But there may be a backlash coming. The strong use of negative ads by Steve Forbes is blamed for hurting his campaign, which began on a very positive note.

The authors fear that independent voters, who are well educated and open-minded, may be so repulsed by the ads that they will become nonvoting apathetics, a great loss to society.

Easy Acceptance

Yet there is little criticism from within the world of political operatives who find political ads on television the easiest, quickest, if not the cheapest, way to reach the electorate.

Tom Edmonds, a successful consultant who has produced political television ads for top Republicans, including Reagan, believes that in the marketplace of ideas the truth about false political advertising will come out from newspaper and television "reality checks." But he is probably overly optimistic about the system. Too many people have been trained to believe what they see on the tube, and this includes political advertising.

The men and women who write and produce these ads, and their colleagues involved in other aspects of the political battle, are becoming a vocal factor in the game—more so than some politicians think is proper.

"If you didn't have so many damned consultants and so many damned polls, it might be easier" for politicians to do their job, claims Democratic House member David Obey of Wisconsin. David Sawyer, a Democratic Party consultant, agrees; "They often have too much power, all ceded by the politicians."

Ed Rollins, a former consultant to Republican Governor Christie Whitman, became nationally famous when he claimed that he had spent a fortune in "walking around money" to throttle black voter turnout in her race, only to later say that he made it all up.

Whatever their individual fame, the consultants are becoming as essential to the process as the candidates. Lately, they have begun to groom their candidates intellectually as well as physically. Where once they merely carried the politician's message to the public, they now increasingly invent the message, and train the politician to carry it forward.

The message or the style may not truly reflect the politician, but in this era of nonintegrity, it's not important as long as the gullible public will buy the image as authentic.

The paradigm of this type of idea-molding consultant is Dick Morris, the éminence grise in the White House. In recent months, he has been super-active in changing President Clinton's style, and reputation, from one of a frustrated liberal-leftist to a centrist who can win reelection.

Morris, a forty-seven-year-old who began in politics as a New York West Side liberal, has shown himself to be politically ambidextrous. He worked with President Clinton in his first victory as governor of Arkansas, then again in 1982 in his "comeback" after a defeat.

Since then, however, Morris has followed the buck. For the last several years he has mainly advised Republicans, including Trent Lott, conservative Republican Whip in the U.S. Senate, a strong critic of the President.

During 1995, Morris became a true power in the Oval Office, where he now insists that the President make every possible patriotic and conservative gesture to win over the center. The "Stealth Strategist," as the *New York Times* dubbed him, has even successfully advised the President not to fight the Republicans on a balanced budget. He persuaded the President to take the initiative away from the Republicans by claiming he wanted the same thing, even in seven years, if with a somewhat different agenda.

Morris has even managed to have the President come out for voluntary school prayer of a type and for school uniforms for children. Under his guidance, Clinton even told (supposedly ad lib) a Houston business group that he had "raised their taxes too much." To erase the image of the President as a draft-dodger, he has pushed him into appealing to veterans' groups and attending war memorial ceremonies, even speaking to such conservative groups as the Veterans of Foreign Wars (VFW) and the American Legion.

Hollywood Remake

This type of ideological rearranging of the candidate for an upcoming political campaign harks back to old Hollywood movies, but it is swiftly becoming a reality in the hands of today's operatives.

In the case of Republican candidate Bob Dole, the message was to appear right-wing in the primaries and more centrist in the general elections. And even more important in image-rearranging, to quell the theory that Dole was a Darth Vader character underneath it all.

Dole was advised to stop scowling and to smile a great deal, as if he actually *liked* campaigning. One sage piece of advice was to take advantage of his age and maturity, rather than become defensive about it. He is casting President Clinton as an errant adolescent lacking seasoning. But to be impartial, Dole's makeover is not nearly as ingenious or dramatic as that of the President's.

Unfortunately, Morris is surely the wave of the future. He is a man who works facilely for either party, as long as he receives enormous rewards, which are rumored to be in the seven figures. He is a masterful style and idea *technician* who can provide the images needed for election.

Integrity, to him, or to those political clients who yield to his blandishments, is meaningless, something that belongs in a prior age. Today, it must yield not only to polls and focus groups, but—and this is the most important factor—to DECEPTION as well.

These are not Democratic or Republican facades. It is all part of a massive American trend, one which is making politics less authentic, less honest and more the product of theater.

We can offer solutions to lobbyist intrusion, as I have. We can rearrange and reform the campaign finance system and the political structure, as we soon will. We can even deal with the curse of television political advertising, and we shall.

But when it comes to consultants taking over the prerogatives, the mind and the integrity of the political system, the nation is on its own. It must gain the skill to discern truth from falsity and see through the scrim that professional operatives are trying, too often successfully, to pull over our eyes.

Now on to our reforms: the first is a "Modest Proposal," and for those with the courage to dream I also offer a "Radical Proposal" designed to remake, reform and rejuvenate American democracy.

8

A MODEST PROPOSAL

Amending the Constitution: More Democracy and Clean Campaign Financing

We have seen some of the problems affecting America, many of which seem intractable and unsolvable. But quite the opposite is true.

What is the key that can solve the dilemmas that confound us?

Simply more and better democracy. As I have said, the people have a natural wisdom far deeper than that of our professional politicians. It merely needs to find an outlet in our complex system.

But why change anything? Weren't the Founding Fathers infallible?

They were for their time, when *indirect* democracy was the foundation of the Union. Since 1787, we have moved closer to *direct* democracy, adding such reforms as the popular election of senators and presidential electors.

We must now leap ahead. Today, only true, direct democracy and an open ballot will do.

To provide a more perfect Union *politically*, we require a new amendment to the Constitution—Number 28—which will establish better laws to organize our democracy. In seven different sections, it will not only eliminate many of the ills that plague the body politic, but reshape the election system. (Amendment 29, to reform campaign finance, will follow.)

The first change has to do with the Electoral College. Because of it, our presidents are not constitutionally required to garner a majority of the popular votes cast. Nor do candidates for any office in the land (except in a few instances such as congressional races in Georgia) need a majority to be elected.

That problem bedevils us in several ways. The 1996 presidential elections offer a sharp insight into some of those failings. It will surely include three or more candidates and the vote will be so split that no one will receive a majority.

The same was true of the 1992 race in which Clinton took only 43 percent of the popular vote, yet was inaugurated as president with 68 percent of the Electoral College.

It's an age-old problem. Eleven American presidents failed to receive a popular majority and three men elected president had actually lost the popular vote—an intolerable situation that must be changed.

AMERICA IS THE ONLY COUNTRY AMONG

THE WESTERN DEMOCRACIES THAT DOES NOT REQUIRE ITS HIGHEST ELECTED OFFICIALS, INCLUDING GOVERNORS AND PRESIDENT, TO RECEIVE A MAJORITY OF THE VOTES CAST.

In the parliamentary system, if no party receives a majority, they form a coalition with another group, amending their own program somewhat to incorporate the politics of the smaller group.

In those nations that have strong presidents as well as parliaments—such as France—many people run for the top office. In the last French presidential election, there were *eight* candidates. The leading ones, François Mitterand, the Socialist, and Jacques Chirac, the Gaullist, did not fear the six others, because according to French law, a majority is needed to win. In the second phase of the election, the top two vote-getters competed in a run-off, and Chirac was the winner. That final cut assured a majority.

Our system is quite the opposite and much weaker. Because we do not have runoffs for President, it actually penalizes everyone involved. The smaller parties have little chance of accumulating a large vote because they are considered "spoilers." People fear those votes will be "wasted."

Conversely, major party candidates actually fear third and fourth party nominees because they will take votes away from them and thus diminish their chance to win.

As a result, the true will of the people is never properly expressed.

Mr. Dole became panicky at the apparent entrance of

Mr. Perot's Reform Party into the 1996 presidential race. Likewise, the Democratic candidate, President Clinton, feared the entrance of Ralph Nader under the Green Party banner. In America, unfortunately, we think of any party other than the traditional two as cutting into the established system rather than adding ideas and vibrancy.

As long as we have the Electoral College and the absence of a runoff, that ridiculous situation will continue. Thus I propose this change in our Constitution, along with several others designed to improve our democracy. The new amendment follows:

28th Amendment to the Constitution

Be it resolved that following a two-thirds vote in both Houses of Congress, and ratification by three-fourths of the states, that the Constitution be amended as follows:

Section One. Method of Selecting the President and Vice President.

The present Article Two, Section One of this Constitution, which establishes the method for the election of the President of the United States, is hereby amended. Henceforth, the Electoral College will be disbanded. The President shall be elected entirely by the popular vote cast, on a national, not state-by-state, basis. The person who receives a majority of the votes shall be named President. If no one receives a majority, a second election shall be held exactly twenty-eight days after the first election solely between the top two vote-getters.

The person who wins that election shall be named President of the United States. The same shall be true for the Office of Vice President.

We must also reform the presidential primary system, which, as we have seen, is a crazy quilt that often sends voters down strange byways of caucuses, closed primaries, open primaries, and state conventions—confusing everyone.

In the Republican primaries of 1996, several holes in the system were exposed. The xenophobic New Hampshire primary ("We're first in the nation," natives boasted) became a travesty of democracy. Money flowed in from all over the country and personal campaigning began a year beforehand. People in that state, used to the new "tradition" of their specialness, demanded that presidential candidates not only shake their hands but make speeches to a crowd of one dozen or less, and pander to their exaggerated local egos.

In that hothouse political environment, where voters felt their vote was more "important" than in other states, Mr. Dole was defeated. Within weeks, however, he easily took the nomination once the exaggerated publicity of that first primary wore off.

The present system is too chaotic, and should be made simpler as part of Amendment 28.

Section Two. Unify the Presidential Primary System.

This amendment shall create a national primary system for all party nominations for President, as follows:

All duly constituted political parties shall hold their primary for President of the United States on the same day throughout the nation, the second Tuesday in March of the year in which the presidential election shall be held.

No delegates shall be chosen for the party convention. Instead, a national popular election shall be held in which only registered members of that party may participate. Any candidate who receives a majority of the votes cast shall be the nominee of that party.

Should no one receive a majority, a second election of the top two vote-getters shall be held on the first Tuesday in June. The winner of that race shall be the party's nominee for President.

This amendment will also solve the seemingly intractable fight over term limits. Since the Supreme Court has ruled that states cannot limit the terms of congressmen, that reform will be included in this same amendment. It will be extensive and conclusive, virtually ending the reign of professional politicians throughout the nation.

Section Three. Length of Terms for Officeholders.

Henceforth, without exception, except for the President, whose term has already been limited by the 22nd Amendment to this Constitution, the terms of all officeholders in the nation, including the state, county and local level, shall be limited as follows:

Executive branch officeholders, including Governor, Mayor, County Executive and all others, though not specifically listed herein, shall be limited to two terms of no more than four years each. Legislative officeholders at the state and federal level shall be limited to serving a total of six years in office, except for United States Senators, who shall be permitted to serve two terms of six years each.

These restraints shall apply throughout the nation but shall not bind a person seeking election to a position that the person has not held before. The restraint is not retroactive, and will begin at the time this amendment has been properly adopted as per Article V of this Constitution.

One of the great tussles in modern America is *us* v. *them*, the perennial battle of the voter against entrenched politicians, who are usually unwilling to give up any of their party or elected power, including the ability to increase taxes. In the Progressive era at the turn of the century, several states shared power with the people by granting them the rights of Initiative, Referendum and Recall.

The Initiative, in which voters may place a proposed law or state constitutional amendment on the ballot by petition, exists in twenty-four states. However, only five of those have been added since 1918.

Increasingly, politicians have hardened their stand on granting further rights to the voters. In Connecticut, repeated attempts by reform groups to put through the Initiative have been rebuffed by party bosses. In several states, specific Initiatives passed by the voters were even amended by the state legislature.

The Referendum, in which the voters may demand to approve or reject legislation, exists in some form in the Initiative states, while the right to recall an elected official by a dissatisfied citizenry exists in only seventeen states. (In one state, Colorado, voters must approve any tax increase through a Referendum.)

To grant these rights to all Americans, instead of to only *some*, the 28th Amendment will include a provision to make them universal.

Section Four. Expand Democracy in the States.

To secure the rights of Initiative, Referendum and Recall uniformly among the several states and its citizens, the Constitution is hereby amended as follows:

Each state shall provide to its citizens the right to place legislation or an amendment to the state constitution or local charter on the ballot through petition. States may set the number of signatures required for same, but in no case shall it exceed 5 percent of the total vote cast for Governor in the prior election.

Each state shall provide to its citizens the right of Referendum, that is the right to approve or disapprove of a piece of legislation passed by the state legislature. Such Referendum shall be placed on the ballot at the next election by petition of citizens, the number of signatures to be set by the

state but in no case shall it exceed 5 percent of the total votes cast for Governor in prior elections.

The right of Referendum shall be granted to the citizens of all states without the need for petition when the legislature has passed a proposed amendment to the State Constitution or has passed a proposed increase in taxes.

The citizens of all states shall have the right to recall any elected official by offering a petition to place such proposed recall on the ballot for the following election. The state may set the number of signatures to place the Recall on the ballot, but in no case shall it exceed 15 percent of the votes cast for that office in the prior election.

Another failing of certain states is that they do not provide for a direct primary for many offices. In Connecticut, potential candidates must seek the approval of party officials and/or delegates to a state or local convention, an example of poor democracy. Voters within a party should make all decisions on nominees, but since some states resist this reform, that change must also be made part of this amendment.

Section Five. Ensure Direct Primaries for All Candidates for Elected Office.

The registered members of all political parties shall have the uncontested right to choose the nominees of their party for all offices, federal, state and local, on a direct basis through a state-sponsored direct primary election. Such nominees

shall have to receive a majority of the votes cast. If a runoff election is required, it shall be completed by the second Tuesday in July.

One method that politicians use to keep ordinary citizens and third parties off the ballot is to make the number of signatures required excessive.

In order for an outside person to secure a place in the political life, the number of signatures required must be drastically reduced in many areas of the nation. In Florida, the requirement for 200,000 signatures and the payment of $20,000 effectively blocks most opposition. In some states, it takes thousands of signatures to qualify for a run for the federal House of Representatives, while in Ohio it is only fifty.

The Constitution must be amended to make all elections, whether for Congress or the state legislature, accessible to all citizens whether or not they are active members of a political party.

Section Six. Open the Political Process for All Candidates for Office.

The state may set the number of signatures necessary for a candidate to appear on the ballot of his party, but in no case shall it exceed the following formula, based on the number of votes cast in the prior election for that same office:

For the contest to choose a member of the federal House of Representatives: no more than one quarter of one percent of votes cast for the office

in the last election, but in no case shall it exceed five hundred signatures.

For a contest for United States Senator: no more than one quarter of one percent of the votes cast for that office in the last election.

For all state and local offices: no more than one quarter of one percent of the votes cast for that office in the last election.

Another problem in American democracy is twofold: States often block the creation of third, fourth or fifth parties and do not have a solid mechanism for people outside the parties to run for office. In many states, smaller parties are actively discriminated against. In Connecticut, our model of bad government, a party that does not secure 20 percent of the statewide vote loses its rights as a major party!

Further, rigged elections such as in many Connecticut towns for boards of taxation, local councils or boards of education, which are not truly contested or counted in conventional ways, will have to be outlawed.

Section Seven. Stop Discrimination Against Minor Parties and Individual Candidates.

Individuals who are not members of a political party shall not be discriminated against in any way when they seek public office by petition. They shall have the same rights as any nominee of a political party.

Nor shall any state make any rules that favor

> **one party over another, nor shall there be designations of "Major" or "Minor" parties.**
>
> **No state shall sanction any election in which the result is apportioned between or among political parties or where voters are asked to choose from a list of candidates larger in number than the positions to be filled (as in "Choose four of the following eight"). All elections must be individually determined.**
>
> **A majority of the votes cast shall be necessary to win elective office at all levels of government. If no majority is achieved in the original election, a runoff shall be held no more than twenty-eight days later.**

These seven sections of Amendment 28 will go a long way toward improving democracy in America. The next step is to reform campaign financing, a task that will never be adequately done by simple legislation, either in the Congress or in the state legislatures. That requires a constitutional amendment as well.

Most everyone understands that money is corrupting the American political system. Too much money is involved in elections, and as the amount raised and spent increases each year, favors—implied or explicit—are increasingly exchanged for that money, making political whoredom more the rule than the exception.

And as the cost of campaigns escalates, politicians spend more and more time raising money and less and less on the public's business.

Everyone speaks of campaign finance reform, and

several bills are now contemplated in Congress. But that activity is futile since it depends on the *voluntary* cooperation of candidates in limiting their own expenditures.

Even if the bills pass, they will have little long-range effect for several reasons. One is the 1976 Supreme Court decision in *Buckley* v. *Valeo*, which ruled that candidates can spend as much of their *own money* on their campaigns as they wish, and that the government cannot limit the cost of any campaign without the candidate's approval.

As long as the system merely *asks* politicians to restrain the cost of their campaigns—no matter the supposed inducements of matching funds and discounted television advertising—the amounts raised will rise and corruption will increase.

That Supreme Court decision was, of course, a ridiculous edict. But until it is reversed or eliminated, there is little hope the nation will ever have a clean campaign system. Meanwhile, the advantage to monied candidates increases.

While others are being encouraged to hold back, the rich have the freedom to spend $1 million, $10 million, $100 million, even $1 billion of their own money. That makes absolutely no sense and must be stopped immediately.

The only possibility of true reform is a constitutional amendment which will change all the finance rules, and put legal restraints on the raising and spending of money in political campaigns. If a democratic people cannot control the rules of their elections, there can be no true democracy.

To stop the moral disintegration of American politics, we must pass still another constitutional amendment, Number 29, designed to create a clean, practical campaign finance system for all candidates for office. Properly executed, it will greatly improve the political environment.

29th Amendment to the Constitution

To provide for a more equitable manner of financing political campaigns at all levels of government, the following amendment, once passed by a two-thirds vote of both Houses of Congress, and ratified by three fourths of the states, shall establish a system for the financing of all political races in these United States.

Section One. Eliminate the Right to Spend Unlimited Sums for One's Own Campaign.

Henceforth, individuals running for public office will not be entitled to spend an unlimited amount on their own campaigns, nor will they be able to borrow monies for such use. All candidates for public office will be bound by limits on campaign financing outlined herein, or passed by Congress within the following guidelines, and shall be able to contribute to their campaign only those amounts permitted to other individuals.

Once that problem is solved, the next objective must be to cut down the total amount of money involved in campaigns. Presently it is some $1.5 billion for all candidates—federal, state and local—in the presidential election years, which is perhaps five times as much as the system needs and should countenance.

The easiest way to reduce the campaign cash flow is to eliminate all other sources of contributions except those permitted by individual adult citizens.

Section Two. Restrictions on Contributions to Candidates for Office.

The following restrictions shall apply:

No corporation or association, profit or non-profit, shall be permitted to contribute any funds to any candidate for public office.

No political action committees (PACs) shall be permitted to collect or contribute money to candidates for public office.

Only individuals of voting age may contribute to candidates, at the following levels:

1. **$250 for elections that are not federal or statewide in scope.**
2. **$500 for statewide elections and for any races for the House of Representatives or the United States Senate.**
3. **$1,000 for candidates seeking the office of President of the United States.**

Those amounts shall apply for each of the primary and general elections. Congress shall have the right to periodically increase these amounts but not at a rate greater than that of inflation.

No candidate may permit any other organization to solicit these funds for them, nor may any group "bundle" such contributions.

Under this new system, the only monies the candidate may receive are from citizens of voting age, and only in the amounts shown. But what about political parties, who now receive upwards of $500,000 in single contributions of "soft money" from wealthy individuals and especially from corporations? All of that must be stopped.

Section Three. Restrictions on Contributions to Political Parties.

No corporation, nonprofit organization, association or political action committee may contribute any money to a political party.

The only contributions allowed are those from individuals and in the same amount as outlined in Section Two of this Amendment. Exceeding those amounts in any one year shall carry criminal penalties to be established by Congress.

Some nationally known candidates get much of their funds from such centers of finance and business as New York, Chicago, Los Angeles or Miami. In a proper democracy, the raising of campaign funds should be restricted to those who have an opportunity to vote for the candidate.

Section Four. Geographic Limitations on Contributions to Candidates.

All monies raised for candidates shall be received from citizens residing as their primary

home in the jurisdiction in which the candidate is running for office. Except in the case of the Presidency, no money shall be raised, directly or indirectly, outside the state in which the candidate has a primary home.

Only candidates for statewide office such as Governor or United States Senator may raise money throughout their state. Candidates for the federal House of Representatives as well as state legislators and local officials will be restricted to raising money only within the jurisdiction involved.

No monies may be received by the candidate from political parties operating outside their own state, nor may such political parties outside the state expend any money on behalf of the candidate.

One election gimmick that circumvents the present election law is section 24E (made famous by the "Willie Horton" commercials), which permits "independent" voters not connected to the candidate to spend an unlimited amount of money on the candidate's behalf. This is the most ridiculous of all present regulations and must be eliminated.

Section Five. Elimination of "Independent" Campaign Spending.

No individual except the candidate himself may conduct campaigns or raise or spend money to aid his election.

Critics will carp; some will even continue the fallacious argument that money is equivalent to "free speech" in the political context. Others will defend the ignorance of our Supreme Court, whose method of interpretation of the Constitution often approximates the accuracy of a Ouija board.

But in the final analysis, the people of a democracy have the right—in fact, the obligation—to ensure that their elections are fair and clean. *Only* the 28th and 29th Amendments to the Constitution that I have outlined in this chapter will provide that environment.

In fact, it is possible that we can advance democracy even farther. Toward that end, I recommend that those of stout heart and agile mind (and Jeffersonian principles) at least consider my Radical Proposal, which follows.

9

A RADICAL PROPOSAL

A Plan for an Ideal Democracy

We Americans are a strange lot. We carp about the failures of government, and occasionally rise to such a point of anger that we do something about it. Then, just as rapidly, our ardor for change cools and we adapt to what is, assuming that there must be merit in the system if it survives.

In the prior chapter I offered many changes in the form of two constitutional amendments (28 and 29) that would, though modest, make a significant change in the way our democracy works. (Other changes involving Congress and lobbyists have preceded these concluding chapters.) If these reforms should be passed, much of the cynicism that now pervades the citizenry will start to vanish.

But once that was done, what if we were to go beyond those reforms and design an *ideal* system?

What if we were to try to advance our democracy by such leaps that virtually all flaws would be corrected and good government would magically appear? Is that too good to be true? Perhaps. But it does deserve an experiment in thought.

If we were to approach an ancient Greek philosopher and ask him to divine the best possible system for a free people, how would he respond?

Or were we to approach Thomas Jefferson, and after explaining exactly what has happened over the intervening 220 years, ask the radical sage of Monticello to design an ideal political system for the twenty-first century, what would he say?

I believe I know enough of the mind of the man who wrote the Declaration of Independence to venture an educated guess. I believe he would advocate two major steps:

1. **The elimination of all political parties.**
2. **The elimination of almost all money in politics.**

How is that possible? How could such a system possibly work?

It's really quite simple. Take point number one. As we've seen, political parties were designed for the nineteenth century, and even performed reasonably well into the first part of the twentieth century. They were practical means of organizing people of like ideas, and for communicating with others throughout a vast continent.

Now, of course, communication is no problem, and people do not have to be organized to express their views. Therefore, the parties are expendable.

We can easily do without the modern party politician. The word "hack" has been correctly associated with many politicians because of their professionalism, their strict adherence to the dogmas of their party and their insistence on raising vast sums of money for their election or reelection.

In such an environment, statesmen are rarely found. In fact, the word is becoming an oxymoron in the present narrow-minded political environment.

Reluctant Votes

Increasingly, most people vote only reluctantly for party candidates, feeling left out of the two organizations whose platforms, ideas and operations are often extremely partisan. In today's complex world, individuals running for office must swallow too much party dogma.

Even worse, once elected, they generally must go along with party discipline or face possible opposition in the next primary. It is because of party mob rule that the conscience of individual politicians is stifled.

Those compromises are excessive and harmful to democracy.

What about the Democrat who believes that thc present welfare system is an abomination and must be scrapped? What about the pro-choice Republican? What about the American who sees the complexities of issues, and knows that policies as outlined in my Middle-Class Manifesto should be adopted, yet feels bound to party allegiance?

People are beginning to understand that dogma is not the answer to most of our problems, and that free thought is required to express the truth in the halls of Congress, in the fifty state legislatures, in the White House itself.

This does not mean that there is a third party, or a fourth, or a fifth, which encapsulates the truth. No, what it means is that there is *no* party capable of understanding and handling all the issues.

Therefore, the logical answer is to eliminate political parties, at every level of government and every level of officeholder, from mayor to president.

Instead, we should rely on the honesty of intelligent nonpartisan citizens, who will come together, issue by issue. It is a superior concept and I believe one whose time will come. If not in this decade, surely in the next.

How would a nonparty, nonpartisan political system work?

It would be quite simple. Anyone who wanted to run for public office would get the required number of signatures as outlined in Amendment 28, then have his or her name placed on the ballot. No party designation would be placed next to their name because there would be no parties.

(Of course, we have the sacred right of assembly and people could always organize themselves into private political parties. But they would have no recognition on the ballot, or legal power as they now have.)

Primaries would be eliminated and a nonpartisan election would be held. The person who received a majority in that election, or in a subsequent runoff, would be the winner.

What would happen, for example, once a nonpartisan Congress was elected by the people? How would it organize and select its leaders?

The same way any nonpolitical institution does—by a ballot or show of hands. But no one would expect party discipline. There would be no party Whips to whip them into shape, no party workers paid by the federal government, as there are today.

There would be no Majority or Minority Leaders in the House and the Senate, because there would be no majority or minority in Congress. The only officials would be the Speaker of the House, and the President Pro Tem in the Senate, who constitutionally are third and fourth in line of succession to the presidency.

End of Party Pressure

Instead, caucuses would come together on specific issues and seek to pass them, unencumbered by "leadership" or party discipline. Then each issue can be truly faced and truly legislated. This principle would apply to the state legislatures as well.

Could Americans get used to such a system?

I think the cleansing of the political atmosphere would be so thorough that the public would feel, for the first time in a generation, that politics belonged to them.

How would we get to know these nonpartisan candidates without a party label, which, while crude, partially describes their beliefs?

As usual, candidates would speak to constituents, appear on television and radio shows, expose themselves to the press.

But there would be one significant change in this system.

To ensure that candidates are well publicized, Congress would pass a law requiring the FCC to require all television and radio stations to set aside *free* time for all federal candidates (with lesser time for state officials) to speak directly to the people, either in debate or personal time. That system is almost universal in other democracies.

But what about paid television and radio political advertising?

That would be eliminated by law. At present, Congress has prohibited cigarette and liquor advertising on television, considering them pollutants of the personal environment. Now it's time to do the same with the third pollutant, political advertising, especially of the doctored attack variety.

Can it be done constitutionally? Of course. The airwaves (not the print media) belong to the public and we can, and have, controlled what is advertised on them.

One boon in eliminating electronic political ads is the savings in campaign money. At present, 40 percent of all political funds go into these electronic media. Cutting them out will considerably reduce the cost of campaigns.

A help? Absolutely. But that leads us into Mr. Jefferson's presumed second suggestion—eliminating almost all money in American politics.

Why should we do that? Because campaign donations are the major cause of corruption, the stimulus for most unethical or criminal behavior. The simple act of politicians begging for money sets up an *unspoken* equation of quid pro quo. (If *spoken*, it's criminal bribery!)

Not that most politicians are unethical. In fact, most are relatively honest citizens. BUT the taking of money by people of such enormous power sets up a system in which not even the politician knows if he's being bribed.

The present need for enormous election war chests is so pressing that self-denial and self-delusion may well be the basic hallmark of politicians, most of whose tin cups are *perpetually* extended.

Perhaps most important, the search for campaign money robs our representatives of energy, sets up moral conflicts many cannot handle and takes them away from the pressing business of an increasingly complex government.

Eliminating Corruption

The 29th Amendment I have suggested will eliminate many of the evils of the money-election system. But in an ideal democracy I believe we must go further and eliminate almost all temptations. That will not only be a boon to a turned-off public, but will be the best thing for psychologically beleaguered politicians.

How would it operate? Again, quite simply. A nonprofit, quasi-governmental foundation would be set up to receive contributions from the public of an unlimited nature. People could contribute in millions, or as little as a dollar, and receive public credit for their effort.

BUT the money would not go to any specific candidate.

Instead, it would go into a central fund and be apportioned for all federal candidates. Each House seat (since all represent approximately the same 580,000 people) would receive an allotment set by law. That amount would be divided among the number of candidates who have qualified for the ballot. They would receive a check, and that would be it. It would be a crime for them to contribute to their campaign or to raise any monies whatsoever.

The same would hold true of Senate campaigns, where a specific amount would be set per registered voter in the state. In the case of the presidency, there would be no more matching funds (except in the signature-filing stage), and each qualified candidate would receive the same amount of money from the foundation fund. No one would be able to raise any money or spend any of their own. Hopefully, states and municipalities would adopt the same system.

Money as a negative ingredient in politics would have disappeared.

The future of democracy rests in our anxious hands. Whether we adapt my 28th and 29th moderate constitutional amendments or seek out the more radical measures, or accept the many reforms I have outlined in this book (or all of the above), something must be done, and rapidly.

America has apparently been endowed by nature, history and the Almighty with a special responsibility to lead the world, in both pragmatic and moral paths. Without a clean and efficient democracy at home, that will become impossible. The beacon that has lit the world in the twentieth century will become dimmed in the twenty-first.

Each of us has a personal responsibility to handle that sacred legacy with care. If citizens and politicians show anything less than the courage and independence needed to maintain a superior democracy, our future—and the planet's—will be jeopardized.

The choice is ours.

ABOUT THE AUTHOR

The Political Racket: Deceit, Self-Interest and Corruption in American Politics is the eighth nonfiction work of author, editor and educator Martin L. Gross.

If follows the publication of his phenomenal bestsellers *The Government Racket: Washington Waste from A to Z* and *A Call for Revolution*, which triggered a national debate on the subject of government spending, inefficiency and the need for true change.

Both books were *New York Times* bestsellers for more than thirty weeks and *The Government Racket* reached the No. 1 position on the *Washington Post* list.

Mr. Gross is also the author of *The Great Whitewater Fiasco*, and *The Tax Racket*.

Mr. Gross has appeared on a host of national television shows including "Larry King Live," "Good Morning America," "20/20," "CBS This Morning," "Prime Time Live," "The Tom Snyder Show," CNN and C-Span to share his investigative research.

The author has testified before the U.S. Senate and the House of Representatives five times on the subject of waste and inefficiency in government, and has recommended many cuts to balance the budget. He has also received thanks from the vice president's office for his revelations, several of which were used in the *National Performance Review*.

Ross Perot has called his work a "handbook for cleaning out the stables" of federal government. He has also been praised by former senator William Proxmire and many other public figures.

The former editor of *Book Digest* magazine, Mr. Gross is an experienced reporter who covered Washington for many years for national publications. His syndicated column, "The Social Critic," appeared in newspapers throughout the country, including the *Los Angeles Times*, *Newsday* and the *Chicago Sun-Times*. His articles have been published in a variety of magazines, from *Life* to *The New Republic*.

The author's prior nonfiction works, including *The Brain Watchers*, *The Doctors*, and *The Psychological Society*, were selections of major book clubs and aroused significant controversy.

Mr. Gross served on the faculty of the New School for Social Research for many years and has been Adjunct Associate Professor of Social Science at New York University.